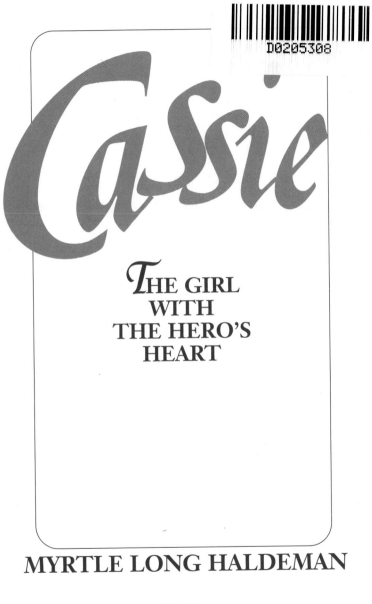

Cassie

The Girl
With
The Hero's
Heart

MYRTLE LONG HALDEMAN

REVIEW AND HERALD® PUBLISHING ASSOCIATION
HAGERSTOWN, MD 21740

This book was
Edited by Gerald Wheeler
Cover design by Helcio Deslandes
Cover illustration by Jack Pardue
Interior illustrations by Elizabet Bame
Typeset: 12/14 Times

PRINTED IN U.S.A.

08 07 06 05 04   8 7 6 5 4

R&H Cataloging Service
Haldeman, Myrtle Long, 1924-
    Cassie: The girl with the hero's heart.

    I. Title.

813.54

ISBN 0-8280-1096-X

DEDICATION

For my nine beloved grandchildren:
Jesse, Rachel, Hunter, Caitlin, Holden, Lucas, Shani,
Harrison, Joshua, and the children of their generation.
To acquaint them with a bit of history
and of life in a simpler time.

This book was written as a tribute to my forefathers and the values they lived by. Elder David Long was my grandfather's oldest brother. He was a highly revered bishop in the German Baptist (Dunkard) Church and a successful farmer. Few records were kept, but I have adhered to all available facts. Many of the anecdotes were passed down through my family.

ACKNOWLEDGMENTS

My thanks to:

My husband, Dan, who labored long and hard at his computer as he transcribed my handwritten word.

Howard Long, a good friend and a direct descendant of David Long, who supplied pertinent facts and family stories.

Ronald Ray Sell, a descendant of James Sell, who granted permission to use *The Historical Church.*

My editor, Elizabeth Lansing, who gave me the courage to complete this book.

My publishing editor, Gerald Wheeler, who fine-tuned this manuscript.

FOREWORD

Cassie: The Girl With the Hero's Heart is a fact-based reconstruction of a real family who lived through the Civil War. David and Mary Long had 10 living children in 1862 and resided on their farm about five miles northwest of the Antietam battlefield. The home and springhouse are still in regular use. Catherine (Cassie in the story) was a middle child about 11 years old in 1862.

Mr. Long had purchased all the slaves at an auction and set them free. His German Baptist Church opposed slavery, and he also felt strongly enough about it to risk the animosity of his slave-holding neighbors.

According to church records, Elder Long preached at the Dunkard church on the Sunday before the battle. And President Abraham Lincoln visited Antietam Battlefield on October 1, 1862.

Family stories passed down through the generations tell about Melvin, his talents, and his physical disability. I have sought to make these historical facts come alive by supplying additional details.

Myrtle L. Haldeman

CHAPTER 1

The large black dinner bell clanged across the farmyard as Cassie yanked the rope impatiently.

It was a balmy spring evening on the David Long farm near Sharpsburg, Maryland. The men were late coming from the fields for supper, for they had to complete spring plowing to prepare the fields for planting corn. They must use all the daylight hours possible to make up for the inevitable days they wouldn't be able to work because of the spring rains.

Cassie watched as the men unhitched the horses from the plows and led them slowly toward the barn. Men and horses were both tired. Since daybreak, Father and her brother Melvin had been walking behind the horse-drawn plows, spelled occasionally by 9-year-old Joseph, who needed all his strength to hold down the plow handles as the blade turned up the soil. Then she hurried into the house, where her mother and older sisters were finishing preparations for the evening meal to feed the family of 12.

"Girls," Mother said, "the men will soon be in. They've had a long hard day of work. We don't want to keep them waiting. They must be half-starved by now. Ella, stir the potpie so it doesn't stick or boil over. Susan, slice your fresh-made bread. My, but it smells good! Fannie, get the apple butter and the pickles from the crocks in the cellar. Cassie, I think the apple dumplings are ready to take out of the oven. After you do that, take the pitcher and run to the springhouse for some fresh cream."

As Cassie leaned down to open the oven door on the big black woodstove the heat slapped her in the face. Thick cloths protected her hands as she pulled the black tins of dumplings from the oven. The sight of bubbling brown syrup and the aroma of hot pastry were almost too much to bear. She quickly deposited the dumplings on the wooden side table and headed out the back door.

From there she skipped down the path to the springhouse. She liked this chore, for she could be in the outdoors that she so loved. The springhouse was a small brick building with a metal roof built over a spring of cold water that bubbled out of the rocks nearby. The water flowed through a channel in the middle of the stone floor.

With its coolness and damp odors, the springhouse was a favorite place for Cassie. Cans of milk, crocks of butter and cheese, and fresh eggs each had their special place either in the flowing water or on the floor of the springhouse.

Cassie lifted the six-quart metal cream can from the shallow water. After removing the lid, she carefully poured the thick, yellow cream into the stoneware pitcher. Then, after closing the heavy wooden door and climbing the three stone steps to the path, Cassie balanced the pitcher on her head, holding it with both hands, as she had seen pictures of women doing in biblical times. Her body straight, she stepped carefully along the path.

The men had already arrived at the house by the time she returned. Father removed the gray granite dipper from the hook on the wall and dipped cool water from the wooden bucket into the basin. After scrubbing his face energetically with his work-worn hands, he used more dippersful to pour over his sweaty neck, head, and beard. Grasping the long coarse towel hanging on a nearby nail, he enjoyed a quick massage and relief from the heat and grime. With the comb from a nearby shelf, he smoothed his beard and combed his hair back from his face. Melvin and

Joseph followed, using the harsh homemade lye soap to remove any stubborn soil, and imitated their father's ritual.

Silently the family assembled around the long wooden table. Mother and daughters had already set the steaming food there ready to eat. As delicious aromas tantalized both young and old, Father folded his hands and bowed his head. Perfect stillness reigned as each one followed his example.

"Our heavenly Father, we do thank Thee for this day. We thank Thee for sunshine and rain from heaven—"

Cassie squirmed restlessly as the prayer continued on and on. When she heard "and bless this food and the kind hands that prepared it—," she knew the end of the prayer was near.

Heads raised as one with the final "amen," and a sigh of relief passed around the long table.

Beginning with Father at the table's head, the food passed from one to the other around the table until all had received an ample portion. Soon the comforting texture and flavor of homemade bread and potpie satisfied the hearty appetites of the growing and hardworking family. A final finish came with bowls of hot apple dumplings smothered in thick fresh cream. At a quiet look from Mother, Ella and Susan left their chairs and cleared the table. Father pushed back his chair, folded his arms, and looked intently around the long table.

"Mother Mary and my children," he began, "some changes need to come. The boys are good workers. Melvin hustles like the best of men. Joseph does his part. Still the work does not move fast enough. We have two more weeks of plowing and we'll need a week for planting corn. Corn should be in before the fifteenth of May. We simply must have help. Tomorrow I will drive to the slave auction."

Shocked expressions crossed each face as they returned his gaze. Mrs. Long's eyes were downcast as she folded and unfolded her hands in her lap. Furrows appeared on her brow. But she asked no questions, made no comments.

Cassie noted the sober looks as questions flew through her own head. Unmindful of her mother's submissive air, Cassie broke the silence around the table.

"Father, what is a slave auction like? I thought you said we don't believe in slavery. Why would you buy slaves? May I go with you?"

Mr. Long's thin lips tightened. His eyes were stern as he replied, "Children should keep silent." Pausing briefly, he continued, "Melvin and Joseph will be plowing. The farmwork must proceed." Turning his gaze on Cassie, he said, "Cassie, a slave auction is no place for women and girls. You are needed here at home to mind Victor and Orville. I will go alone."

No one else said anything. Cassie, not easily intimidated but with voice trembling, said, "I know I might be the only girl there, but I'd be with you. I want to know about slaves, and why people are fighting about slavery. I wonder how the slaves feel. Do they have feelings like ours? Are they people like us?"

Her father stared at her silently for a moment, then began to smile at his young daughter, who was forever asking questions.

"You have an inquiring mind, Cassie," he said at last, "and that's good. It's not a pleasant thing, a slave auction, but if you must know about it, you might as well go with me. We'll leave at 7:00 in the morning."

Cassie's mind raced as she thought of the exciting day ahead. Oblivious of all else, she absentmindedly wiped the dishes as her sister Fannie washed them, and thought about how much she loved her father for giving her such a privilege. She remembered the times when she and her father walked the farm together. His occasional chuckles told her better than words that he loved her quick mind and her endless, sometimes impertinent questions. Even though he silenced her sternly at times, she knew it wasn't the questions that concerned him, but the customs that they must follow.

Why, she asked herself, *should children keep silent? Why don't mothers ask questions? There's so much that I don't understand. I want to learn about life, about people, about growing up. Sometimes I feel so grown up. Other times, I feel like a little girl and don't want to grow up. Grown-ups are so serious and work all the time. Mother never stops working. She always seems tired. Even Ella is looking old and hardly ever smiles, and she's only 19.*

Fannie gets that dreamy look in her eyes and I see a little smile curving her lips, even when she is washing dishes. She's strange! 'Course Lizzie likes to help Mother in the house and sit around with needlework. What a bore! I don't understand her at all! I'd much sooner be outside.

The dishes done, she hurried out the kitchen door toward the barn. There she collected a bucket of warm milk, which she carried to the lamb pen. She sighed contentedly. Four little lambs rushed up to her, bleating plaintively. Setting the bucket of warm milk down, she nuzzled each one as they pushed and shoved for a place at the bucket.

Cassie watched the lambs with a feeling of tenderness as they greedily sucked up the milk, wiggling their tails, butting each other playfully, and letting forth an occasional "ba-a." Chin in hand, she sat with her long, plain cotton dress pulled down over her knees and sweeping the ground. Frequently she reached out and gently petted the lambs' springy, short wool. As their tummies filled, the lambs came to her for more petting. Next, they competed for room as they awkwardly tried to leap onto her lap.

Lambs are such fun, Cassie thought. *I do love them so much! I could watch them all day frisking about and playing together. But it's getting dark. I must be sure the lock is tight on the door so no dogs or other animals can get in. I'd want to die if anything happened to the lambs.*

With that, she stood up and said, "Good-night and sleep tight, little ones. I'll see you in the morning."

As the moon appeared in the eastern sky and the last rays of sunlight faded in the west, Cassie strolled toward the house, wondering again what adventures awaited her the next day.

Entering the kitchen, Cassie saw everyone already engaged in an evening activity. Mother and the older girls were sitting with their needlework, Father was reading, Melvin was whittling as Joseph watched, hoping to learn how, Julia was playing with her doll, and Victor had his marble game. Orville, almost 2 years old, was sleeping peacefully in the big cradle.

Mr. Long looked up as Cassie opened the door. With eyes twinkling and a gentle smile, he said, "So you've been with those lambs all this time, Cassie? Do you think you can leave them tomorrow? They'll be baaing for you all day."

"Oh, they like Joseph, too!" she answered. "They won't miss me that much!"

"You'd better go on to bed now," he said. "It'll be a long ride and more excitement than you're used to. You'll need your rest!"

Cassie said good-night and heard some vague "G'nights" in response. She climbed the long back stairway to the little bedroom she shared with Lizzie and Fannie. It was cooler now. Quickly undressing, she laid her clothing out neatly on a chair, ready to slip into in the morning. Wasting no time, she slid her soft cotton nightgown over her head and climbed into the high rope bed. The thick feather tick felt cool and soft. She knew she was tired as her head sank into the thick goose-down pillow. *But I'll never go to sleep,* she thought. *I'm so excited!*

Soon she tossed fitfully. All the terrible things she ever heard about slaves and masters and beatings seemed to rush into her dreams. Once she cried out, "No! No! It hurts!" Was she the one being hurt or was it someone else?

CHAPTER 2

Time to get up, Cassie." Her mother's gentle voice called up the stairway from the kitchen. Wonderful breakfast smells swept through the open door.

Cassie made a flying leap from her bed. A hurried glance out the window and she saw the sun climbing above the horizon. Quickly she slid into her clothes, then leaped down the stairs two steps at a time. She dashed into the kitchen and rushed to her surprised mother with an energetic hug and kiss.

"Oh, Mother, how can I help? I'm jumpy as a leap frog. Thank you for letting me go with Father. I'll be very good. I can hardly wait to get started," she said breathlessly.

Her mother smiled at her baffling young daughter. Why Cassie would want to go to a slave auction was more than she could understand. *Of course, but then she's always been a tomboy,* she thought.

"Of course you can help. We'll need cream from the springhouse for the grits. Then you can take the wild honey from the cupboard and pour some into the honey pot."

Thoughts of hotcakes swimming in wild honey made Cassie's mouth water as she hurried off to the springhouse.

Returning with the cream, she heard the men's voices as they neared the house after the morning chores. Up since 5:00, they had already completed the morning work of feeding cows and horses, milking the cows, and cleaning the stables.

While Father and Melvin did their usual cleanup ritual,

Mother and the girls finished preparing breakfast. A large pot of oatmeal and a bowl of brown sugar came first, with a pitcher of cream at each end of the table. They kept the hotcakes warm on the stove shelf.

More children came tumbling downstairs, sleepy-eyed, enticed by the tempting smells.

Soon all were seated around the long table. Father asked Melvin to get the family Bible and read a passage for family altar. Melvin chose Psalm 103, reading clearly and with feeling.

I wish he had chosen a shorter one, Cassie thought as butterflies of excitement winged through her head, though she did try to keep her mind on the words.

Finally Melvin ended, and closed the large Bible reverently. Father bowed his head, and each head lowered accordingly. The prayer was long and inclusive. Thanks, praise, family members, neighbors, work, business of the day—he mentioned them all. No one and nothing was forgotten. The children sat quietly with heads bowed and eyes closed throughout the prayer. Cassie found it especially long today.

At the close of the prayer Mother dipped out the bowls of grits, and soon breakfast was under way. Hotcakes followed. A hearty farm breakfast would supply the energy they needed for the hard day's work.

"If you're ready, Cassie, it's time we be going," Father said. "The horses and spring wagon are ready and waiting by the hitching post."

They said goodbye to the family, climbed onto the wagon seat, and with a loud "Giddap" started on their way.

It was a glorious morning. Birds warbled as they flitted through the trees. The sun spread its magic over the countryside, showering nature with hints of gold. A slight breeze stirred as nature awakened. Squirrels and chipmunks scurried about. Rabbits hopped from one green morsel to another, nibbling greedily, but wary of enemies lurking about.

The roadway was bumpy as the large metal-covered wheels rolled along. The horses chose a rapid gait, eager for a good run. Mr. Long restrained them with a tight hold on the reins.

"Father, why did you decide to go to the slave auction? I thought we didn't believe slavery is right. Are you planning to buy slaves?" Cassie questioned.

"Daughter, there are many hard decisions that grown-ups need to make. It's true, I believe slavery is wrong. It is a peculiar institution, started thousands of years ago. We read of it in the Bible. Many have accepted it as the way to make a living. The more slaves you own, the more crops you can produce and the more money you can make. No farmer can afford to pay a living wage for the work that needs to be done. Especially cotton farmers, where so many things must be done by hand.

"Our church believes slavery is wrong. Why should one man own the body of another? Sometimes it seems he owns the soul as well. And some masters are very cruel. Half-starving their slaves, they give them one-room, dirt-floored, rat-infested shacks to live in. They expect them to work daily from sunup until after dark. And they hire overseers to whip them mercilessly. There has to be a better way!"

"Then why are we going to an auction?" Cassie persisted.

"I must have help. It's too much for Melvin and me. Joseph is still young. There are many mouths to feed. I plan to buy several slaves and set them free. If we treat them well, I believe they'll want to stay with us. It may make trouble, though. Some of our neighbors have slaves and won't like what I'm doing. But we'll just have to live with that."

They rode on in silence.

As they drove onto the site of the slave auction, they saw other spring wagons approaching. Some had already arrived and their drivers had tethered their horses. Other people carried buckets of water from the town well to water their horses after a long trip.

Cassie

Cassie noticed the men milling about, dressed in farm clothes of coarse homespun and wearing heavy cobbled shoes. Some were chewing tobacco with the brown juice dripping over unkempt beards. Others puffed serenely on curved pipes, while still other men had chosen the more potent aroma of foul-smelling cigars.

Such gatherings allowed neighborhood news to be shared, weather and spring planting discussed. It was a chance to compare and keep abreast of the surrounding world.

As slaves appeared on the platform, the men's attention began to focus there. Occasional raucous laughs rang out as someone made crude comments about the slaves.

Cassie noticed that the slaves were dressed in clean clothes and appeared well, but looked terrified. She turned to her father. "Why are they dressed so nice and clean, yet look so frightened?"

"The owners want a good price for them, so they make sure they look their best," Mr. Long replied. "The slaves do not know what will happen to them. They fear the worst. Nothing is so degrading as to be brought out like cattle, sometimes stripped of clothes, and made to show their teeth or have their flesh pinched by would-be buyers."

Cassie frowned, many thoughts chasing through her mind. Then a horrible one filled her head: *What if I had been born to slave parents? I could be standing up there for sale.*

The auction began and the auctioneer called the group to order to announce the proceedings.

As Cassie watched, one of the men roughly pulled a young girl to the front of the platform.

"Oh, Father, there's a girl about my age. Look how she clings to her mother!"

"She's afraid she'll be sold away from her family," he explained. "Many families are broken up by being sold to different plantation owners."

"But, Father, how can they be so cruel? How terrible to be taken from her parents and never see them again! I've heard people say that some young girls are abused by their owners, too."

"Yes, daughter, it's sad but true. Slaves are created by God, as we are, and should be treated as equals."

Cassie looked at the young girl. Head down, eyes downcast, the child was shaking with fright.

Suddenly they heard the crack of a whip.

An auctioneer's helper leered at her as he said, "Dance, girl! Show what 'ya got!"

Unsmiling, eyes rolling in fear, she waved her arms and did a rhythmic dance with her feet to the sound of an inner beat.

The loud guffaws and clapping from the assembled slave buyers angered Cassie.

"Father! Do something. Don't let them do anything else to her. She's not stupid. She's pretty. She must feel awful!"

"You're right, Cassie! I can't stand this any longer and I won't," her father said as he stood tall, eyes bright.

The auctioneer called out, "What am I bid for this young filly? Looks like a top-notch kitchen maid. Who'll bid $75?"

"One hundred dollars," Cassie's father shouted.

All eyes turned toward him. Why would anybody jump the price like that for a mere child? She couldn't be worth more than $75.

"One hundred dollars I got. Who'll raise it to $125?" the auctioneer shouted.

The men stood silently and looked confused. No one else offered any bids.

"Sold! To David Long for $100," bawled the auctioneer.

"Oh, thank you, Father. Now I know she'll be all right," Cassie whispered.

The auctioneer's helper grabbed the trembling girl roughly and led her to her new owner.

19

Cassie smiled at her as the girl stood meekly before Mr. Long.

"Is that your mother up for auction?" Cassie asked her softly.

Head down, the girl nodded a yes.

Cassie tapped her father's shoulder. Their eyes met.

A stern intensity burned in her father's eyes as he saw the woman now on the auction block.

Again the auctioneer's voice sang out, "What am I bid? She's young. She's strong, a dandy buy."

The helper circled the woman, pinching her flesh.

"Two hundred dollars!" Mr. Long yelled.

Again confusion as the men muttered to each other. What was going on?

"Sold for $200—to Mr. Long!"

Someone yanked the woman off the platform and shoved her toward Mr. Long.

Cassie smiled happily as mother and daughter held each other close.

The woman looked furtively at Mr. Long as a man Cassie instantly knew to be her husband was pulled roughly to the auction block. Previous beatings had left bloody welts on his back. Sweat poured from his forehead as he cowered before the auctioneer.

Cassie tapped the girl on her shoulder.

"Your father?" she asked softly.

A quick nod gave her the answer she needed. She pulled at her father's sleeve. As their eyes met, she whispered, "Him, too—her father!"

Without hesitation Mr. Long placed his bid. No way should families be separated. He would not allow it.

Shortly an auctioneer led the man stumbling over to join his family. He raised his head just enough to peer into the eyes of his new owner, then straightened a bit as warmth and compassion met his gaze.

The auction continued, and so did the pattern.

As soon as a slave was offered, Mr. Long made a high bid, discouraging any further bids.

He purchased six slaves in all.

Cassie and her father led the way to their horse-drawn wagon. As Cassie climbed onto the seat beside her father, the slaves crowded into the back.

As they drove off, Cassie sat quietly, thinking about the girl her father had bought. *Can I really be a friend to her? Can I be fair to her? Nobody else is. What will my friends think and say? She doesn't talk as we do. Nor can she read or write. I'll just have to try.*

The ride home was quiet and uneventful. It was midafternoon, the warmth of the sun increasing the easy peace. Trees were greening, the fields sported moss-green covers of wheat, and occasional flocks of birds broke the expanse of peaceful azure sky. Snowy clouds, drifting lazily, added to the serenity.

Mr. Long halted the horses near the big oak tree at the edge of the yard.

"We'll unload here," he said. "I have some important things to tell you. Cassie, go get a bucket of water and a dipper from the springhouse. After that long ride, we're all thirsty."

Cassie ran to the springhouse and soon returned, carrying a heavy bucketful of water in one hand and a dipper in the other.

Mr. Long took a long draft from the dipper, then filled it again and handed it to the first slave to his left. The bucket and dipper passed from person to person. How good the water tasted as it slipped down dry dusty throats.

As Cassie sat on the grass by the roadside she looked thoughtfully over the group of slaves. *That dipper, passing from one to the other, reminds me of an Indian peace pipe. I wonder if it means the same thing.*

Standing with arms folded and a gentle smile, Mr. Long addressed the slaves.

"My brothers, today begins a new life for you. You are no longer slaves, but free men. Today I will begin the process of securing your freedom papers. That means you will have a choice. You can stay with me and work where you are needed. I'll provide food, clothing, and a home for you. I can't pay much, but I will give you a small wage. Or, you are free to go when you receive your papers. No one will hunt or return you. You can choose where you want to live and work."

Looks of surprise and disbelief crossed everyone's face. Their heads, usually bowed, now raised. Eyelids, half closed, opened wide. Sober, fearful looks became almost smiles as they stared at their benefactor. Clearly, they were wondering whether he really meant to set them free. They listened closely as he spoke again.

"I have given you a choice. I stand by my word. How many of you choose to make your life with us?"

Without hesitation all six slaves raised their hands in loyalty to the man who promised them freedom. Broad smiles creased their faces and they hugged each other. In exultation, one slave shouted, "Hallelujah, praise the Lord! We be free at last!"

A wild clapping of hands followed.

Mr. Long smiled broadly. "Well, friends, there's work to be done. The sun will be long with us. We must get on with the spring plowing. But first, it's food we all need. Cassie, go tell Ella and Susan to bring out some corn bread for all of us. A couple of pitchers of milk and tins from the springhouse will wash it down real well. We can't work with our stomachs growling."

The slaves smiled and chatted happily as they wolfed down the corn bread, followed by long drafts of cold milk.

"Seems time to get acquainted," Mr. Long said finally. "You know me, but I don't know your names."

He nodded to the first slave.

"I Ephrim."

"I Mose. This is m' wif', Sally, and our girl, Mandy."

"I Renty."

"Me Jack."

Mr. Long studied each one thoughtfully as he considered ages and capabilities.

"Cassie, take Mandy and Sally to the kitchen," he instructed. "Your mother will know what they should do. Come with me, men," he added as he started toward the fields. "One of you can relieve Melvin at the plow. He's been trailin' that horse since daybreak in spite of his one short leg. Mose, it'll help you forget your painful back when you get a whiff of that sweet-smelling loam where the plow cuts through. Renty, Melvin'll show you into the barn. You hitch up Bessie and man the other plow. Pick up the furrow on the other side of the field."

Turning around, Mr. Long started back toward the house and the small field behind the springhouse. "Jack and Ephrim, we'll go back and start laying out the truck patch. Spring's a growing time, so the sooner we get seeds planted, the quicker we'll have fresh garden victuals on our tables. The root cellar is nearly empty—just a few dried-up apples and half-rotten heads of cabbage. The meat in the smokehouse and the grain from the mill are about all we have to go on until garden things come in.

"The women will take care of the kitchen garden. They're probably itchin' to get out of the house these warm sunny days. The hayloft in the barn will serve as your beds until we have cabins built. It shouldn't take long with all you good men to help."

CHAPTER 3

My, what a palace we live in now!" Mama Sally exclaimed as she and Mandy cleared away breakfast. "I has to pinch myself every day to believe our wondrous good luck. Even the haymow in the barn was better'n that old shack we used to live in. Now in just two weeks, this cabin with a kitchen, a bedroom, and a loft place for you, Mandy. It's too much! Thank the Lord!"

Her face shone like black satin. With arms upraised, she joined hands with Mandy as they did a joyful dance. Out of breath, they fell into their chairs laughing.

"They sure did build this cabin in a hurry," Mandy said. "Our men just wouldn't stop working. Papa looked just glowing when it was all done. Miz Long was so good to Papa, putting that stuff—what they call it?—petroleum jelly on Papa's sore back. Made him like a different man. Now he can't wait to get over breakfast and get out there to them fields to work."

"Yes," Mama Sally said, "I don't believe I can soon forget the days on the old plantation. That overseer, he was one mean man. I'll never forget those whippings. 'Most every day somebody got tied up to a tree with his face against the bark, arms tied tight around it. Then he'd take that long curling whip and bring the blood with every lick. Folks all over that plantation could hear them awful whippings. They was a terrible part of living. When it was your papa's time, I just went in the shack and sobbed and cried so loud I couldn't hear it.

"The next day the boss man come tell us we was going to auction. 'Needed money,' he said. Thought our trouble couldn't be no worse. At them auctions we'd be sold like cattle. Families be split apart, children sold one place, mamas another, and papas still another. Maybe never see each other again.

"'N' now we be free. I wouldn't even care if I was a slave for Mr. Long. He be so kind and Miz Long so gentle and good. I just wanna praise God all day for bringin' us here."

Remembering the pain and now her unutterable joy, Mama's face was radiant. Light seemed to envelop her entire being—or so it seemed to Mandy.

"Guess I'll go find Cassie with the lambs. She needs help with those little bitty ones. They just climb all over her, sometimes even knock her over. But she just laughs and gets back up. She be a true friend. I never had a friend before. Sometimes she so serious, wants to know everything. I just say, 'Stop worrying, Cassie. It's grown-ups got to worry. We might just as well have fun before we get grown up.' Then off we go giggling 'n' laughing about the silliest things. Feels so good inside to have a friend."

Mandy hurried out of the cabin, the door slamming behind her. A quick run to the barn and she found Cassie sitting among the lambs, petting with one hand and pushing them off with the other. Loud, plaintive, continuous ba-a-a-s signaled their urgent needs. Two bucketsful of milk sat outside the pen. Mandy knew Cassie couldn't manage to feed them all alone. She unlatched the gate, picked up the buckets, and held them high as she neared the frisky lambs. Just one overeager lamb's quick butt could tip over a pail of milk. That lesson she had quickly learned. After handing one pail to Mandy, she moved to the side of the pen with the other pail. The lambs slurped noisily.

"That little black one is a nosy fellow," said Cassie. "He's little, but he looks out for himself. I bet he gets more than his share."

"He pushy, all right," Mandy agreed. "He not gonna starve. Bet he be the biggest one in another month."

"They all look pretty sturdy now." Cassie nodded toward a small lamb. "I did worry about that wee one at first. She just didn't want to drink any milk, not even licking it off my fingers. It made my heart sad to see her so weak. I was remembering my little brother who died last winter. He was Orville's twin. It was such fun to see the two of them together, even though it was hard to tell them apart. And then they got sick. Mama tried so hard, and we all took turns holding them, putting cool cloths on their faces to chase the fever, flannel mustard plasters on their little chests, and giving them sips of warm broth. Finally, Orville's fever dropped and his eyes brightened. But Wilmer only got weaker and wouldn't take even a sip. He just got paler and weaker.

"Then one morning Father told us before we got up that Wilmer died during the night. We all cried. Mother was brave. She said, 'We'll all miss Wilmer, but we thank God that we still have little Orville.'"

Mandy looked soberly at her. "I so sorry. If he was cute as Orville, it must have nearly broke your heart."

They finished feeding the lambs quietly. As the animals frisked about in play, the girls slipped out the gate and walked thoughtfully toward the house.

"Hurry up, you two," Fanny called from the porch. "Mother's been waiting for you. You sure don't seem to be in a hurry."

"Oh, that Fanny," Cassie exclaimed. "She'd like to see me get into trouble. I think she's jealous because we're friends. Lizzie's so quiet and the other girls are older, so I guess she'd like someone special to share secrets with, too. Sometimes she gets that faraway look in her eyes and her lips turn into a half smile. I wonder what she's thinking about. She seems to forget what she's doing."

"Maybe she's getting sweet on boys," Mandy suggested

with a dimpled giggle. "Girls her age start acting queer, especially round boys. I don't know why."

The big kitchen was a beehive of activity. Ella was rolling pie dough on the side table. Susan was darning socks in a far corner. Mama Sally was making up the fire to heat the oven, and Mother was shelling peas.

Each day had its routine of chores for the large household. Monday was wash day, Tuesday was ironing, and so on through the week. Always there were cooking, cleaning, mending, and other endless needs to be met.

"Mother, what is it you'd like us to do now?" Cassie asked. "Mandy and I just finished feeding the lambs. They really need lots of attention."

"I'm sure they do, Cassie, and I know you and Mandy give them the best of care. Right now, there is so much to be done. I need you girls to gather dandelions for dinner—a big dishpanful—and then pick the strawberries before the sun is so hot. After that, there'll be the butter to churn, so try not to dilly-dally too much."

Taking the big dishpan between them and kitchen knives for digging, the girls were soon kneeling on the lawn searching for tender green plants.

"What was it like, Mandy, living on a plantation with lots of other slaves? Did you have other girls to play with? Do you miss your friends?"

"Weren't anything like here. Had to help Mama in a hot kitchen all day. Women folk there was ladies. They didn't work. Just sat around looking pretty. There was a girl about my age. She didn't want to be friends. She want waitin' on hand and foot. And it was me did the waitin'! 'Get my shoes, Mandy, comb my hair, Mandy, bring water for my bath, Mandy.' All day long! Run up and down steps, in and out the kitchen, 'n' all the time needin' to help Mama. There be some girls work in the fields, but they not very smart. Mama didn't want me to 'sociate with them.

"Workin' in the kitchen, we got better food, but just left-overs. Mistress helped us if we were sick. Guess she didn't wanta lose her cooks." Mandy laughed.

"Didn't you ever have any fun? How could you work all the time?"

"Oh, some Saturday nights we sang and danced when Renty and Jack play banjo and fiddle. Everybody come out and have a rollicking good time. Sundays we all went to church and sang and shout a lot. That feel good, too. Then nice afternoons Papa would take me fishing while Mama wash clothes and clean the cabin. All she want was just to rest a bit."

Sharp eyes and nimble fingers soon filled the dishpan and carried it to the kitchen. Smiling approval, Mama Sally handed them the berry buckets.

Buckets swinging, the girls headed for the strawberry patch. It was a favorite task. Pick two, eat one, pick two, eat one—the biggest and the juiciest. No one would ever know. After feasting on the luscious berries, they looked at each other's red-stained mouths and fingers and laughed.

"What a sight you be!" Mandy exclaimed. "Guess we better wash in the spring before we goes in. But before we do that, we'd best fill these buckets."

"Right, Mandy. Strawberries don't look so good anymore, so now we can finish our job." Looking up, Cassie asked quietly, "Mandy, why do you keep on talking that way? You're plenty smart. Why don't you start talking like we do?"

"Why should I? Mama don't, Papa don't. All Blacks speak this way. If I change, they think I uppity, trying to be like Whites. I'd only bring me trouble. Don't need that." She sobered and shook her head.

"Well, I wish you could read. Reading is really fun. If you'd try, I could teach you and lend you books."

"Don't care about reading. Couldn't go to your school any-way. 'Course, I don't need to read. I hear them stories you read to Julia and Victor—know them by heart already. Why trouble myself?" she answered, rolling her eyes mischievously.

"Guess you're right," Cassie agreed reluctantly.

The moist, cool atmosphere of the cellar was a welcome change from the baking heat of the sun in the strawberry patch on a June morning. Cassie and Mandy took turns wielding the handle of the big barrel churn. Cassie, puffing a bit as she neared the end of her stint, joined Mandy in a chant as the rich cream slapped the sides of the churn.

> "Come, butter, come
> Come, butter, come
> Johnnie's at the garden gate
> Waiting for a buttered cake
> Come, butter, come
> Come, butter, come."

With a final flourish of the handle, Cassie dropped to the dirt floor, exhausted. The two friends laughed together as they exchanged places—Mandy at the churn and Cassie seated on the overturned basket.

The only light was from the glow of the candle in the pewter candleholder. The flicker of the flame cast eerie shadows in the dark corners of the cellar. Scuttling sounds in the gravel added to the eerie feelings. The dampness crept in on them like noise-less cats' feet. Mandy shivered as she began her shift.

"Why is this butter so slow?" she asked impatiently. "Seems like it's taking forever!"

"Maybe we're just tired," Cassie answered. "I'll be glad for dinnertime and some good strawberry shortcake. We've really earned it."

The girls continued their labor and their song. Finally a *thud-thud-thud* sound came from the churn.

"It's coming, it's coming!" they both shouted happily.

They dashed up the rickety cellar steps to report their success.

"Butter's done!" they announced importantly.

"Good!" Mother replied. "We're just ready for dinner. The men have come from the fields and are already washing up. The butter will wait for working and molding until after we eat."

Since meals were a time for family talk, they had set up a separate table on the porch for the help for at least the summer. Each held ample food. Big slabs of hickory-smoked meat, boiled potatoes, fresh dandelions with vinegar dressing, concluded with strawberry shortcake and cream.

Dinner over and chores finished, Cassie and Mandy called Julia, Victor, and Orville to join them for a walk in the woods.

They all went down the path past the springhouse. Only Orville slowed the pace of eager feet. They paused just long enough to splash the cool springwater on their hot faces.

Holding Orville's hands between them, the two girls gently urged him on. After being inside all morning, he loved the out-of-doors with its warm breezes, scurrying wildlife, and twittering birdsongs. Julia and Victor trotted ahead, eager for adventure but secure in their awareness of Cassie's and Mandy's presence. Their little brother Orville was always around in the house. At least now outdoors they could keep some distance between him and them.

They all trudged over the fields through rows of green corn plantings and along the edge of the waving yellow grain. The split-rail fence slowed them only briefly as they either climbed over the top or slid easily between the rails. The earth was soft and spongy under their feet after the abundant spring rains.

As they entered the big woods a huge silence greeted them. Layers of wet leaves and moss formed a springy carpet underfoot, interspersed with squishy wetness that oozed in through the cracks of their thin worn shoes. Twigs from over-hanging branches caught in their already tangled hair. Picking their way around trees and between saplings on a scarcely visible path, the children plunged on. Cassie and Mandy led them while protecting little Orville from swaying branches above and footfalls below.

Finally they heard the wonderful sound of swishing, bubbling water as it tumbled over rocks and rippled downstream. They hurried toward it, now slipping, now half falling on the rough path.

Slipping hastily out of their shoes, they dipped their feet into the cool water, then stepped into the stream. Letting go of Orville's hand and tucking up her long skirt, Cassie headed farther into the water. It felt wonderful as it swirled around her. Stepping cautiously on the slippery stones, reeling from side to side as a sharp stone dug into her foot, Cassie plowed on, unmindful of the rest of the children.

Mandy watched as Cassie floundered ahead. Dropping Orville's hand, she began to tuck up her skirt. Julia and Victor were busily pitching stones along the edge of the stream.

Orville toddled forward to reach Cassie. Suddenly, as Cassie took still another step, her foot touched nothing. Overbalanced, she fell forward into what seemed to be a bottomless hole. Flailing her arms and sputtering, she planted her feet firmly on the stream bottom, relieved to find herself only waist deep. As she turned to find her companions, she saw Orville. Reaching toward her, he toppled into the big hole and disappeared.

Eyes wide with terror, she screamed for Mandy. They joined hands while Cassie groped for the child. Sliding one arm under his armpits, she pulled him upward toward her. Blinking and spitting, the boy broke into a wail as his head rose out of the water. With Orville clinging desperately to Cassie while Mandy steadied her, they climbed shakily out of the water toward the stream edge. Speechless, they sat down on the nearest rock, both girls seeking to comfort the frightened little boy.

"Do you think he's all right?" Mandy finally asked.

"I hope so," Cassie said miserably.

CHAPTER 4

Morning in mid-September 1862 was beautiful in the Cumberland Valley south of Hagerstown. Cool nights with a hint of frost had turned the summer's harvest into autumn's glory. Vast fields of corn were changing from summer green to autumn brown while masses of goldenrod lined the fence rows. The fruity smell of apple orchards laden with near-ripe fruit and the peach trees readying for winter seemed to say, "All's well."

Breakfast was long past for the field hands. By rising with the sun they had gained an afternoon of freedom. "Sukey, Sukey" came the sound of cattle calls from the pasture. It was milking time and the cows were ready for their breakfast of grain. Another farm hand was already behind the plow, shouting at the horses, urging them on as they plodded lazily. With a joyful bark the sheepdog gleefully herded the flock toward the barn. From the woods came the rasping sound of a crosscut saw and finally a crash as a large dead tree crashed to the ground. It would make a heap of firewood for winter.

The tranquillity of this scene totally belied the inner gnawings of fear and dread that clutched at the hearts of the people. Anxiety now tightened the once-smiling, contented faces of young and old.

The smoke of battle, already sighted on nearby South Mountain, brought reality to the doorstep of the Long home.

Reports of a battle at Harpers Ferry reminded them of a war in progress.

Around the breakfast table there was more talk than usual. Mostly questions. Might there be a battle here? Were their lives in danger? What could they do to be safe? Would there be soldiers on their farm, shooting at each other?

Since Maryland was a border state, it meant that the Rebels were coming from the south and the Union soldiers from the north and east from Washington, D.C. Already they had heard terrible stories from other parts of the country of stolen horses, barn burnings, homes laid waste, and a winter's food supply stolen. They looked at each other in wide-eyed fear.

Mr. Long bowed his head. "Dear Lord, thank You for Your help in times past. Take our fears and give us wisdom for the coming days. Amen."

Like fleecy clouds floating in a blue sky, a feeling of calm settled into the hearts of each one. Mr. Long spoke and everyone listened attentively.

"Dear ones, I wish I could say that all will be well. I cannot. We must trust in the Lord. He will guide us in the coming days. We cannot hate, we must not fear. We must regard all men as brothers. This is our Lord's teaching. I understand that some families are divided. While some fight for the Union, others fight on the Confederate side. That means that some brothers will be fighting against brothers.

"It is a sad day. We do not believe in war. We will not fight. We will seek to love and serve.

"Soldiers will be hungry. We will share our food. Many will need shelter. We have a warm barn. Whatever they feel a need to take, we will willingly give them. At the same time, we need to care for our own.

"Our barn is bursting with a plentiful harvest. The cattle are fat from the good summer pasture. The smokehouse is crammed full. A first kettle of apple butter has been boiled and stored in the cellar. We have enough for our family and more to share.

"The cabbage and small potato crop that were buried underground and covered with mounds of straw need not be disturbed. Melvin and I will bring meat from the smokehouse. Some we will leave there. Susan and Fanny can hide the others in the secret attic above the fireplace. We must safeguard our winter's food supply.

"Now, we will prepare for the Lord's Day. Mother Mary will need the help of all of us to prepare food for tomorrow. I expect to call a meeting here at our home in the afternoon. Since our house is the largest in the community, we will invite all our friends and neighbors to discuss together how we can prepare for the soldiers' coming. And I believe they will. As we meet and plan together, we will receive comfort and strength from one another."

Mr. Long rose from the table, donned his straw hat, and strode out the door. Melvin and Joseph followed.

"Mommy, will you be here when the soldiers come?" little Victor asked.

"Yes, dearie, I'll be here as always, cooking and caring for the family."

"Then it's all right. They won't hurt me if you're here."

Mrs. Long smiled at the easy trust of her small child.

Already Cassie and Fanny had cleared the table and washed the breakfast dishes. Some chores were routine and quickly completed. Today, though, time was precious. They looked to Mother to direct their work.

"Girls, we must not waste any time. We'll need to kill, dress, and cut up 10 or 12 chickens for frying, gather and prepare vegetables from the garden, bring in apples to peel for applesauce, and bake an extra week's supply of bread. Then we'll be needing at least three cakes and 10 pies baked. Of course, the folks coming will bring food, too, but we need to be prepared for hungry soldiers, as well.

"Ella, I'll turn the bread baking over to you. You'll need an early start. Mama Sally will be in charge of the chickens. Fanny, when you're finished with the meat, you can pick the apples and start peeling. We'll need a half bushel at least. Lizzie and Julia can come with me to the garden. Victor, you can help us gather, too. Cassie and Mandy have their barn chores. Then they can help as needed."

Cassie and Mandy flung open the kitchen door and raced each other to the barn. They knew their cows were waiting to be milked. Molly, Cassie's favorite cow, was mooing loudly as the girls looked over the half door into the stable.

"Sounds like old Molly is getting impatient," Cassie said. "I guess her udder is about to burst, it's so full. It shouldn't take long to fill my bucket."

"Her moos sound a little mad to me," Mandy replied. "Her big brown eyes be rolling 'round not so friendly. You'd best be careful, Cassie."

"Oh, she'll calm down as soon as I strip her out a little."

The girls unlatched the stable door and walked across the straw-covered dirt floor. Mandy pinched her upturned nose as the mingled odors from the gutter reached her nose.

"I be glad when we finish this job. Those men didn't get this stable cleaned out yet. Sure smells revoltin'."

"My, my, you really are one prissy miss, Mandy," Cassie teased. "You'll look funny holding your nose with one hand and milking with the other."

They giggled.

"Never you mind. Bet I be finished my two cows before you," Mandy retorted.

Rushing, they bumped each other as they grabbed for their clean pails and then again as they pulled their three-legged wooden stools from the shelf.

Mandy was seated by her cow in seconds.

Cassie laid her hand on Mollie's flank to gentle her. The cow turned to face her with quizzical eyes.

After placing her stool in position, Cassie set her bucket under Molly's bulging udder and then sat down, tucking her long dress up under her. She began squeezing and pulling on two teats with long slow strokes. The streams of milk hit the metal bucket bottom noisily. Her strong young arms moved faster and faster. Soon her bucket was half full of warm, foaming milk. Molly looked at Cassie calmly. Then in one swift kick, the cow's foot was in the bucket. Over the bucket turned, causing the milk to spill into the straw bedding and run into the gutter.

"Oh, Molly, how could you!" Cassie scolded as she jumped up, her dress dripping milk. Molly looked at her smugly.

Too late Cassie realized that the rough place on Molly's teat was a fresh scratch that hurt when squeezed.

Barn chores finally finished, the two girls went to the feeding entry and climbed the ladder to the haymow. It was their secret place. By burying themselves in the mounds of hay they could share secrets, both happy and sad, with no fear of being seen or heard. Today was one of those times.

"I'm scared, Mandy; are you? There's like a rock in my stomach that won't go away."

"Yeh, I scared, too," Mandy replied. "It's been so peaceful-like all the time we be here. Now most anything could happen. I see a coupla them Union men coming 'cross the field when we left the lamb pen."

"I guess that's the beginning. Probably more will be along after them. We'd just better stay close to the house and the grown-ups. Like Father says, we'll need to be kind and share our food."

"I be scared 'cause I Black. Most White men don't treat Black girls like White girls. I really afraid," Mandy said quietly.

"Remember, Mandy, we're friends, and we'll stick

together. If soldiers come to the house it's better that you hide so they don't know you're here."

Reassured, Mandy turned her attention to some soft purring sounds nearby. "Do you hear those purrs, Cassie?" she whispered. "Bet that mama cat has her kittens hiding round about here. Let's look."

Stealthily, the girls climbed out of their hay cover and began inspecting the dark corners of the haymow. A pair of green eyes met their gaze. A mass of little bodies tumbled about over the mother cat as they searched for warm milk. The girls dropped to their knees and watched them.

Dingdong! Dingdong! sounded the dinner bell.

Both girls leaped to their feet.

"It can't be dinnertime already," Cassie said, catching her breath.

"Bet it's for us. We been out here a long time. We'd best hurry in to help."

As they raced to the house, they saw Fanny standing on the porch, hands on her hips and a frown on her face.

"It's about time you two show up," she said. "I can't peel all those apples myself. I bet you were playing around again, and us with so much work to do."

Neither one said anything, even though they ached to tell about the kittens.

Going into the kitchen, they saw Mother stringing beans.

"It did take you a long time at chores this morning, girls. Now, I think Mandy better go help Mama Sally with the chickens. Cassie, you will help Fanny with apple peeling."

Meekly the two friends hurried to their assigned tasks.

Mandy found her mother near the chicken house, where the chickens were squawking loudly.

"Those chickens real upset," Mama Sally said. "Guess each one wonders would she be next. Melvin just finish' chopping off those heads. Now we has to scald the rest and pluck out the feathers. I been boiling lots of water for all these chickens."

Mandy plucked fast and clean, eager to make amends for her lateness.

Noon and dinnertime came quickly. It was a welcome rest from the long morning's work. The aroma of frying chicken, bread baking, and spicy apples cooking greeted them at the kitchen door. Platters heaped with meat, baked beans, and fresh brown bread made a feast.

Quickly the family assembled around the table, offered prayers, and swiftly emptied the platters. As hollow stomachs filled, there came a lull. Mary Long looked up and spoke quietly.

"Father, we're going to need more food supplies. There's not much flour left in the barrel. We'll need more for baking each day. Plus sugar for cakes and pies and coffee."

"Very good," Father replied. "A trip to the gristmill and the store is possible this afternoon. It's important to have plenty of supplies on hand. Melvin, you can help me load up several bags of wheat and corn for the gristmill. We'll catch a dozen chickens and take the corn that is left to barter at the store. Cassie and Mandy can bring the young ones with us. The kitchen work will move faster with them out of the house."

Cassie's slight smile barely hid her mounting excitement. It wasn't often that Father let her go to the store. It would be tricky keeping Orville in tow, but with Mandy to help, they'd manage. They could easily keep Julia and Victor out of trouble with the promise of a licorice stick. And Mandy would be thrilled. She'd never been to the store.

Bright smiles creased the children's faces as they stood watching Father and Melvin load the grain and bags of noisy chickens on the spring wagon. They fussed for the best seats on the grain bags, but were soon settled and ready to be off. Father climbed onto the seat and flicked the reins over the horses. With a rattle of wheels and in a cloud of dust they started on their way. The wagon road soon lost itself in the woods beyond the farm.

Mandy's eyes darted about, refusing to let a single sight escape her. She giggled as she spotted a gray squirrel sitting motionless, trying to look like a part of the tree. A rabbit eyed her as it cropped delicate green leaves. Their eyes meeting, it sprang fast away, white tail bouncing through underbrush.

With a hearty "Who-a" and a hefty yank on the reins, Father pulled to a stop at the gristmill. While the little ones jabbered blithely, Cassie and Mandy helped unload the grain. Dropping it at the gristmill, they continued on to the store.

As was customary, local people had gathered at the country store to swap stories and local gossip. Men loafed about outside the store, chewing tobacco and discussing the war. More sober than usual, they considered where they thought would be the next likely place of battle. Some sidelong, disapproving glances toward Mandy only made Cassie walk straighter with her head held high. Mr. Long tipped his hat, smiled kindly, and joined the group of men.

"Have you seen any action yet?" he asked them.

"Haven't heard any close shots yet," one farmer replied, "but the officers have sent some boys ahead to find a good place to set up camp. Guess we'll see more of them tomorrow."

"Probably them rebels are crossing the river now," another said. "We'll be sure to see some bad times the next day or so."

"The Lord be with us all," Mr. Long answered. He left the group and followed the children into the store.

Already, little mouths were happily dripping licorice juice. Mr. Long wasted no time. With Cassie's help he collected a 10-pound bag of coffee beans, 100 pounds of sugar, a pound of nails from the nail keg, and a few smaller items.

"I have two bags of corn and 10 chickens in the wagon," he announced to the store owner. "Will you accept that as an even trade?"

"Even trade," replied the storekeeper with a nod and a smile.

They placed the goods on the wagon and headed back to

the gristmill. There the miller had ground the bags of wheat into flour and the corn into cornmeal. While Mr. Long loaded the cloth bags the children trooped over to watch the water gushing over the huge waterwheel. Leaving such a fascinating experience wasn't easy, but at Father's call they returned to the wagon.

That evening, the day's work done and supper over, the family gathered in the parlor for family altar. Light from several coal oil lamps cast dancing shadows around the large room. Melvin sat at the pump organ matching chords with melody for "Little Mohee." Smiles wreathed the faces of the children. They loved this familiar story song. Led by Melvin's tenor voice, they sang the entire story.

> "As I was out walking
> upon a fine day
> I got awful lonesome
> as the day passed away."

Favorite hymns and Scripture followed. Father, with his warm twinkling eyes and gentle smile, gazed from one to another. "Do you have any concerns or problems you want to tell us? Nothing is too big or too small," he said.

Cassie raised her hand hesitantly.

"At school yesterday some boys were mean to Melvin. They pointed their finger at him and called him Old Hippity-hop. Just because his one foot is shorter and he has to wear that thick-soled shoe is no reason to be laughed at. I was mad at them, but I didn't want to start a fight. They're not near as smart as he is."

"Name-calling is cruel," Father replied soberly. "It's a poor way to have fun. I'm glad you and Melvin let it pass. A forgiving spirit is a sign of grace. There are times we all need to be forgiven. Let us all remember to forgive one another."

The prayers were long with deep feeling. The family sensed a great need and knew the Power that could still their hearts.

The silence after the "amen" was broken only by a gentle snore as Victor's head nodded devoutly.

Closeness and a spirit of peace seemed never more present, but what changes would the tomorrows bring?

CHAPTER 5

Sunday morning, September 14, 1862, the countryside was bright with late summer sunshine. A haze hung over distant South Mountain to the east.

The Long family rose early. Only necessary daily chores were allowed on Sunday. It was a day to dress in their best clothes and then drive to church for services. There they would meet and visit with friends and neighbors.

Cassie and Mandy went about their chores earlier than usual. Today Father would be preaching at the Antietam area Dunker church. Mr. Long preached at several churches nearer home, but Antietam was six miles distant, which required a traveling time of one and a half hours.

They held family altar even though they would be attending a church service, then ate a hearty breakfast in anticipation of the long drive. After they had completed all their morning chores, the family changed into their best clothes.

The sparkling clean carriage and two spring wagons waited in the driveway, each pulled by two farm horses. At exactly 7:30 Mr. and Mrs. Long took their places on the front seat of the black canopied carriage, simple in design but reserved for Sunday use. Behind them, Ella, Susan, Fanny, and little Orville arranged themselves comfortably.

The second wagon, driven by Melvin, carried the other members of the family.

The "help" occupied the third wagon. Mama Sally made

Dunkard Church

sure that all were clean and neatly dressed for this special occasion. The bright turbans Mama and Mandy wore added to nature's colors.

It was necessary to rein in the horses occasionally to avoid the dust that billowed up from the wagon ahead.

Nearing the church, they sighted friends coming from other directions, riding horseback, walking, or in a variety of wagons and carriages. Their hearts tingled with excitement.

The little white-painted brick church, located on a hill overlooking Sharpsburg, nestled among sturdy oak trees. The Hagerstown Pike lay to the east and the West Woods to the west.

One by one the carriages, wagons, and horses arrived on the church grounds. After the worshipers dismounted, men and boys led the horses to hitching posts, tied them securely, and gave them water from the church well.

Cassie hurried over to chat with her friends. Mandy soon followed. As she entered the group, she sensed a sudden quietness.

"You don't belong here with us," Sarah said with an upward tilt of her chin, glancing at Mandy. "You belong with your family."

"Why doesn't she belong here?" Cassie asked hotly. "She's my age and she's my friend."

"Your friend?" Sarah said with a smirk. "We don't call her kind friends, do we, Katie?"

The other girl looked away, unwilling to take sides.

"Suit yourself," Cassie said, "but either she's one of us or we're leaving!"

Rebuffed, Sarah turned aside, directing her attention to the boys huddled in a group a safe distance away. "I wonder what they're talking about. They seem to be having fun. Let's get closer. Maybe we can find out."

The girls inched a little nearer, hoping to hear without the boys knowing.

Pausing, they noticed one boy looking at Melvin. He snickered as he made a comment to another boy. Then, smugly he approached Melvin and asked, "How long was Moses in the ark?"

Melvin thought a bit and answered, "I don't know."

The boys laughed uproariously. Together, they shouted, "Noah, stupid!"

Melvin replied calmly, "Look up Exodus 2:3."

Cassie's eyes blazed momentarily, then her face relaxed into a half smile. *They're the ones that are stupid. Melvin's too smart for them! Won't they be surprised when they look that text up!*

As it was time for worship, Elder [1] David Long led the way through the east door into the church. The men and boys followed him, finding seats on the right. Cassie joined her mother and sisters as they entered the south door and sat on the left facing the pulpit.

German Baptists, commonly called Dunkers, wore quiet colors of black, gray, and blue. The women had modest dresses with high necklines, long sleeves, and full skirts that swept the dust as they walked. They did not use jewelry, considering gold or silver as satanic. Women arrived wearing "prayer veils" or "prayer coverings" made of fine white net. In cold weather they added black bonnets for warmth.

The men wore broad-brimmed black hats that topped rounded haircuts and bushy beards. Their black coats had no lapels but an upright or "standing collar." Black hightop "Sunday" shoes completed their costume. Younger people who were not yet members of the church wore more fashionable clothing.

Today, when the congregation had seated themselves, Elder Long rose from his seat, opened the large Bible, and read from the Psalms. After appropriate comments, he sat down and another elder arose. Since the group did not use musical instruments, they "lined" hymns. Someone would announce the hymn and read the first line. All joined in singing that line. Then the elder read the next line and the congregation sang it. Such "lining" continued for the entire hymn as well as for later hymns.

Elder Long took his place behind the pulpit and began preaching a long and fervent sermon. Often quoting selected Scripture passages, he reminded his listeners of their many blessings of health, family, and abundant crops. Emphasizing the folly of war, the equality of all people, and the need for peaceful settlement of conflicts, he spoke of the brotherhood of all and the sadness of brothers fighting against brothers. No one doubted the truth or the sincerity of his words.

Several times during the long sermon the roar of gunfire from South Mountain shattered the stillness inside the little church. Each time a cannon fired, Cassie shivered uncontrollably. Fearful thoughts played havoc in her mind until she could not bear it. Then she thought of the crowd of guests coming to her home. Warm feelings of friendship and delight in the bustle to follow helped her forget the impending battle.

More hymn singing followed the sermon. Finally Elder Daniel Wolfe stood and called the congregation to prayer by saying, "Let us kneel in prayer."

The congregation knelt on the wide board floor, facing the back of the pew, with elbows resting on the seat. Cassie found the position awkward and tiresome during long prayers. Feelings of guilt assailed her as her mind persisted in wandering.

Elder Wolfe prayed for the North and the South, made a plea for little bloodshed, and prayed for a peaceful settlement. Following the service of several hours, someone dismissed the congregation in the fear of the Lord.

Elder Long made a final announcement inviting everyone to his home for an afternoon meeting and a fellowship meal.

The little church emptied quickly as families left its sacred refuge to face the dangers of the days ahead. Some proceeded to the Sam Mumma farm, which lay across the wheat stubble fields east of and in sight of the church. Others followed the Longs toward their farm.

Several teenage boys lingered to climb the hill to the north of the church. In shocked disbelief they saw long lines of Confederate soldiers, artillery, wagons, and cavalry moving from the town of Boonesboro toward Sharpsburg. Soon after, they spotted a column of Union troops marching toward them.

As the horses and wagons came to rest at the gate of the Long farm, the family hurried inside. Clouds of dust rolled up in the distance, signaling the early arrival of a host of friends. Some were coming in the driveway already.

Mary Long swiftly directed everyone to what they should do, as if she had planned the details throughout the homeward journey.

"Ella, you"re in charge of tables. The men will bring sawhorses and boards to make a long table on the front lawn. We can seat about 50 in the dining room. It will be a tight squeeze, but the women and little children need to be inside on a cool day. The men and older children will do fine outside. Sister Miller said they would stop at their home to collect extra dishes and tableware. There'll be less carrying if we use her things on the lawn table. You can begin setting the table inside now.

"Cassie, you and Mandy help Ella set the tables. Then fill the pitchers at the spring to place on the tables."

Turning to her husband, she continued, "Father, we'll need lots of drinking water. I imagine everyone is pretty dry now. Several milk cans of water on the porch should take care of that."

"You"re so right, Mary," her husband replied. "You're always thoughtful of others. I'm mighty proud that you can feed a crowd like this."

Tables inside and out soon groaned with great platters of food, overflowing baskets of fresh bread, heaps of fried chicken, cinnamon-flavored applesauce, and fresh garden vegetables. Cakes and pies completed the sumptuous spread.

After all were seated inside and out, they waited in obedience for the ritual blessing.

Within the hearing of all, Elder Long raised his hand in blessing and bowed his head in prayer. Deep voiced, he prayed, "Our Father in heaven, we give thanks for each one assembled here and for the abundant food—."

The blessing now over, mounds of food disappeared quickly. Young and old ate heartily. Many wondered whether it might be the last feast before a long famine.

Cassie and Mandy were kept busy moving around the table. They made sure that food got passed and the children received what they wanted. At intervals they checked on water pitchers, refilling them from the large milk cans of water on the porch.

Both girls found the outside table of particular interest. Frequently they found their gaze drawn to the group of young teenage boys. But always they avoided letting the boys know that they were watching them. Cassie took great pride in her ability to carry water pitchers in the biblical way. Today was no exception. It was something she felt she had to do. After refilling a large pitcher, she stepped carefully down the several porch steps and walked demurely toward the boys' end of the table. All watched her. As she approached the table, her attention was diverted to one special boy. For a moment her step faltered.

As she lifted the pitcher from her head, it tipped. Water gushed down on the head of the boy at her side.

"Yowl!" he screamed in sudden shock. The other boys doubled over in laughter.

Cassie turned beet red, set the pitcher down hastily, and dashed into the house.

Mandy pretended not to notice. She understood Cassie's humiliation and realized her friend could not possibly appear outside again.

Dinner over, the women bustled about, wanting to help put the house in order. Iron teakettles of water boiled for washing dishes. The women carried several large dishpans outside. Others gathered leftovers and carried crocks of food to the springhouse. In record time all signs of the meal vanished. The men dismantled the makeshift outside table and returned the boards to the barn.

Children skipped off to shady spots or rambled freely around the spacious lawn, unaffected by adult worries.

Older boys escaped in a ball game, grateful for a way to release their strange mix of feelings. How could one sense fear and excitement at the same time?

The women soon formed little groups in and around the large house, some knitting and some attentive to their needlework. Others, weary from a hard week's work, were content to have time just to sit.

Cassie, relieved of chores, collected her friends in a favorite spot on the lawn. Here she was intent on hearing what the men would say about the approaching battle and the plans they needed to make for it.

The men carried benches over under the big oak tree. Their sunburned faces glistened with streaks of perspiration from the afternoon sun.

Mr. Long began the meeting by saying, "No question but what we'll see a battle, though exactly where we don't know—maybe in our own backyards.

"Soldiers will probably be camping on our farms, killing our livestock for food, and sleeping in our barns. How can we protect our families from maybe hundreds of soldiers?"

Brother Miller spoke up, "The armies use many horses. They always need more, because great numbers get worn out on the march or killed in battle. They'll surely be after our horses."

"Yes, that's true, Brother,[2] but our horses are like ourselves, peaceloving," Mr. Nicodemus responded. "They don't make good war horses. My guess is they'll go after the young horses. At any rate, I'm going to lead as many as I can into our cellar and make sure there's plenty of hay to satisfy them."

"Sounds good to me," Mr. Long said. "It won't be easy getting horses to pass the outside cellar door and down the steps. We'd best tie cloths over their feet to quiet them. Otherwise, the soldiers can hear their stomping in the cellar."

"What of the women and children?" another man questioned "They'll be in danger. Many shells go astray."

"As much as we love our families, we cannot always protect them," Elder Long said. "They must stay indoors, out of the line of fire. We pray our homes will be safe."

The men continued talking in subdued tones among themselves, reluctant to leave.

Finally, Elder Long stood and said, "Brothers, it has been good to be together. We must keep our faith strong!" Raising his hand in benediction, he said, "May the Lord be with us all!"

As he embraced those nearby, others too joined in heartfelt farewells. Tears clouded their eyes as they realized they might never meet again.

Cassie now saw the seriousness of their situation. Grown men didn't cry. She swallowed hard as she said goodbye to her friends.

Then joining her family on the porch, she watched with a heavy heart as the wagons rumbled down the road and disappeared into the woods.

---

[1] In the German Baptist tradition the level of ministry between an ordained minister and a bishop.

[2] The German Baptists, or Dunkers, addressed each other as Brother or Sister.

CHAPTER 6

Monday morning dawned bright and clear. Breakfast over, Cassie, needing no reminders, headed for her barn chores. Mandy soon joined her. Before long they both were in the lamb pen, reveling in the warmth and friskiness of the little bodies.

"It's easy to forget all about the war with the lambs tumbling over us," Cassie said. "I wish nothing would change," she added pensively.

"Yeah, these little fellows don't know about war. They just wanna fill their tummies," Mandy answered with a smile.

"I wish grown-ups would figure out a better way to solve problems. It seems like everybody loses in war—soldiers die, homes are burned, people go hungry. What's the good of it?" Cassie sighed heavily.

"No good a' tal!" Mandy responded, her dark eyes blazing. "Your folks do it the right way. Now we all be happy. Soon we all be afraid and unhappy!" She stomped her foot angrily.

The lambs fed, the cows milked, and the chickens taken care of, the girls walked slowly toward the house.

"Oh, Mandy, I have an idea," Cassie said suddenly. "Why don't we go to the orchard, find the tallest tree, and climb up to watch the soldiers as they come? It will be our secret place, and no one will see us."

"Sure, that be fun! With our work finished early, no one will miss us."

Off they raced to the orchard, the wind cool against their faces, pigtails flying. With a series of boosts and grabbing each other by the hand, they both struggled up into the tree.

Each positioned herself comfortably on a thick branch and leaned back against the tree trunk. Surrounded by ripe, juicy apples, they were soon munching contentedly. Looking to the north, they saw lines of men and boys in blue uniforms approaching in broad columns, some to their right, some to the left. Smoke from campfires dotted the landscape where the early arrivals had already set up camp for the night. The girls watched in fascination. The soldiers looked gallant in their striking dark blue uniforms. Then, too late, they realized that some were approaching the house. Now what should they do? In a few moments there would be no escape from their secret hideout. They eyed each other anxiously.

Acting quickly, Cassie began sliding down from her perch. As small branches snapped noisily, they heard a sudden command.

"Halt!" shouted a soldier. "Who goes there?"

Cassie shrunk back, her heart frozen with fear.

Below her stood a soldier, gun aimed directly toward her.

Shielding his eyes from the bright morning sun, he searched the dense foliage. Seeing two frightened young girls, he smiled, then broke into laughter.

"So you're the enemy!" he chuckled. "Better get down before the other boys get here. They'll eat you alive!"

The girls scrambled down like a pair of startled gray squirrels and raced madly toward the house, sure the whole Union army was after them.

As they neared the kitchen door, a new concern claimed their attention. How long had they been gone? Long enough for Mother to be angry?

They inched through the doorway stealthily. Things were humming in the kitchen. Nobody seemed to notice them.

Picking up courage, Cassie announced, "I think some soldiers are coming to our house. I heard them when I was out on the porch."

Mandy nodded in agreement.

"Dear me, I wish your father were here," Mary Long said. "He must be out in the field. I'll meet them at the door."

A sharp rap on the door followed. Wiping her hands on a coarse linen towel, Cassie's mother, work-worn, weary, and eyes clouded with worry, opened the door.

A cheerful-looking captain greeted her. "My men have been marching since dawn," he said. "Do you have a good water supply hereabouts?"

"Oh, yes. Behind the house—in the springhouse you'll find all the water you need to drink. Do help yourselves!" She smiled in relief.

"We'll be setting up camp for the night in the hay field. Others will be going farther south. We have supplies, but we'd sure appreciate some extra grub."

Generous by nature, Mother Mary assured him that they had food to share.

After drinking their fill of springwater, the 50 or so soldiers scattered about over the front lawn, some standing, some sitting.

The women scurried about in the house frying meat, making huge omelets from dozens of eggs that had been stored in the brine in the big crock in the cellar, and gathering pickles from the pickle crock. They sliced loaves of bread and piled them in a large basket with pounds of fresh butter on the side. Then they carried it all out to the porch and spread it on the table. Jugs of milk and tin cups rounded out the home-cooked feast. Mother Mary was careful to keep some distance between her girls and the soldiers.

The soldiers ate greedily, leaving nothing behind except the empty containers. Some stretched out on the lawn with only their packs for pillows. Others followed the captain to the site chosen for their camp. A few set out to explore what the barn had available for their use.

Mary Long, exhausted, as she prepared to take to bed for rest, said, "They ought not to bother us now that I fed them."

The girls, too, felt easier about returning to their rooms. Only Mama Sally lingered in the kitchen to finish some final cleanup.

She heard the rattling of the back door. Before she knew what was happening, a soldier stepped clumsily through the doorway. Giving her a sideways grin and wavering from side to side, he said, "So the others have all cleared out. That'll give me and you time to get acquainted."

He advanced toward her.

Mama Sally, seeing he had been drinking something besides milk, grabbed a big iron skillet. Cheeks flaming and her eyes large and dark with a mixture of anger and fear, she started toward him, holding the skillet high in her right hand and saying, "You go out that back door and keep a-goin'. Don't you ever set foot in here agin!"

In suddenly sober amazement, the soldier backed off and soon vanished.

With a look of smug satisfaction, Mama Sally went from door to door, sliding the iron locks in place on each one.

As she sat peeling potatoes for the family meal she sang:
> "Keep yo' eye on the sun;
> See how she run.
> Don't let her catch you
> With your work undone."

Cassie had heard the commotion and had investigated. Now she stifled her giggles as she turned again to go upstairs.

Early Tuesday morning the Union soldiers broke camp on the Long farm and marched south toward Sharpsburg. More troops came from the north, some marching in formation, some on horseback, and some in scattered little groups. Tramping through the fields, they broke down fences, stripped fruit trees, and left havoc behind them. Whatever they wanted, they took.

Tension mounted in the Long household. Helpless in the midst of this invasion, they could respond only with grim acceptance. Food supplies dwindled rapidly. The soldiers slaughtered the livestock and loaded it on wagons for roasting at their next campsite. Mr. Long guarded his doorway. When called upon by an officer, he responded calmly and kindly.

Some horses had been lodged in the cellar early Monday morning. Those left in the barn the soldiers hitched to wagons and loaded the wagons with new supplies from the well-stocked farm.

Food and blankets for the family had been stored in another part of the large cellar. It seemed to be the best place to wait out the battle that would soon be upon them.

Around noon a Dunker family that lived near the church arrived at the Long homestead. In a state of panic, as they saw the armies preparing for battle nearby, they had fled their home, thinking they'd stay with relatives in Pennsylvania until the worst was over. But encountering so many marching soldiers, they decided to seek lodging for the night at the Long farm. Mr. Long and Mother Mary welcomed them, ready to share their meager supplies.

All agreed that Wednesday would be a terrible day. The visitors reported that General Stonewall Jackson and his troops had set up camp in the fields and woods back of the church. The forces of General D. H. Hill and James Longstreet were stationed in front.

"Why, the soldiers even milked our cows," the farmer friend said. "General Jackson sent a soldier with a message to General Hill. Before he left, he gave the general a drink of milk from his canteen. 'Straight from old Bossy!' he laughed, when he passed him the canteen."

Later in the day as the Union soldiers began to thin out,

stragglers from the Confederate army wandered onto the Long farm. Long marches over mountain roads without shoes, little rest, and nothing but green corn to eat for weeks had left them a sorry sight. Ragged, filthy, and sick, they aroused great pity in the Long family.

That evening chores were lighter than usual. With horses missing, fields laid waste, orchards empty of apples, not much was left to do. Cassie thought she had never seen Father's face so sad. Because of the broken fences many cows had wandered off. Would they ever return? The men threw hay down from the mow to feed them when they did come back. The half-empty corncrib still held enough feed for the few hogs and chickens left. Little lambs bleated plaintively for Cassie and Mandy. Several older sheep had been taken, leaving motherless lambs.

Cassie and Mandy stacked firewood outside the kitchen door, not knowing how long they'd be prisoners in their own home.

More friends appeared in the evening, sensing a need to get away from the probable battle site. They reported that General McClellan had set up his headquarters on the Pry farm. Soldiers had set up tents, unfurled flags, and driven stakes in the front lawn to support telescopes for observing the battle field. The general had told Mr. Pry, "I expect a big engagement and plan to give Bobby Lee the whipping of his life."

"We drove through both battle lines less than a mile apart," said one friend. "They used our rail fence for campfires to brew coffee and cook maybe their last meal. Some were hunched near the light of the campfire writing letters. They pinned them to shirt pockets or stuck them in their New Testaments. Some notes were given to comrades who might be less likely to be hit.

"Near one campsite we heard voices singing softly:
'Just before the battle, Mother,
I am thinking most of you
While upon the fields we're watching

With the enemy in view.
Comrades brave around me lying,
Filled with thoughts of home
    and God;
For well they know
    that on the morrow
Some will sleep beneath the sod.
Farewell, Mother, you may never
Press me to your heart again;
But oh, you'll not
    forget me, Mother,
If I'm numbered with the slain.'"

Just before bedtime Cassie slipped out of the house and sat on the porch. The sky was clear, the woods hushed. The moon came up so full and round that she felt she could touch it. The air was as still as before a storm. Cassie trembled and said under her breath, "O God, what will happen tomorrow?"

CHAPTER 7

The earsplitting sounds of cannon and rapid gunfire awakened the Long family at an early hour. It was Wednesday, September 17, before 6:00. Unable to sleep now, they dressed and went to the kitchen to prepare an early breakfast.

It was too risky to attempt any outside chores. Some 26 people milled about the big kitchen, anxious to retreat to the cellar for greater safety. Nearly paralyzed with fear as the cannon roared continually, hunger was the last thing they were thinking about. Breakfast soon over, they huddled in the cellar, there to wait out the sounds of battle.

Several hours later a blast shook the timbers of the big brick house. Women screamed, children cried. Men held their lanterns high, but the light revealed nothing changed. No one was hurt, their shelter was intact. They heard no crash of falling walls or timber.

"Thank the Lord!" said Mr. Long in a quiet breath.

By 9:00 the sounds of battle lessened with only an occasional gunshot. Having been packed so tightly in the little cellar room that they could feel each other's breath, it was with relief that they returned upstairs.

Still hesitating to go out into the open, they spread into the living room. Believing the battle to be almost over and feeling restless in the crowded house, the men soon took off for the barn.

Mr. Long, Melvin, and Joseph needed to find out what had caused the terrifying explosion. Inspecting the house from top to bottom as they circled it, Joseph was the first to see the damage.

"There it is, up at the top!" he shouted, pleased to be the first to make the discovery.

The three looked in amazement at the huge gaping hole in the east wall near the roof.

"Must have been a cannonball," Melvin commented. "But why? We're miles from the battle lines. Was it a stray shot or were there different battle locations?"

"We may never know," Father responded thoughtfully. "We were very lucky not to be closer. I dread to think what happened to homes near the battlefield. And the church was right in the middle. I can't imagine what it looks like now." A cloud seemed to cover his face.

"Can we go see it?" Melvin asked, a tinge of excitement in his voice.

"I think we must. But not until we're sure the battle is over. We must wait until the fighting stops. There will be many boys crying for help, both Blues and Grays," he said with a catch in his voice.

The wait seemed long, but as soon as they thought it was safe, the men took two wagons and headed down the Hagerstown Pike toward the Dunkard church. On every hand they saw property destroyed, broken-down fences, cattle chasing about like wild deer, and the remnants of campfires. Along the way they saw a group of farmers milling about in confusion like a flock of hysterical hens in a henhouse after the visit of a chicken thief.

Stopping the horses, the Longs approached the group. They saw glazed and bloodshot eyes in men dazed from the sound of battle. The rattle of musketry had benumbed their senses. Yet they were glad to see friends and share news.

"What of the battle?" one man asked. "Is it over?"

"No, it's only moved farther south. If only we'd see the end of it!" another farmer responded.

"What's the tall pillar of black smoke down the road?" Melvin asked.

"That's what's left of the Sam Mumma farm," someone replied. "The Rebels were staying there and were driven out by the Yankees. To make sure the Yankees couldn't hide there, the Rebels set fire to the whole place—house, furniture, clothing, barn, grain, hay, and farm equipment. It's all gone but the clothes on their backs. I hear the Mummas have gone to the Sherrick farm to stay."

Some said the Mumma daughters, Lizzie and Alice, didn't want to leave. When one of the Southern soldiers offered to help them over the fence, they turned their backs on him, too angry to accept help.

A gray-bearded farmer added his story.

"The Yankees were complaining that the Rebels had put salt in the Mummas' springwater, and it wasn't fit to drink. Later, someone asked Sam about it. Sam said, 'No, my father was in Hagerstown on Tuesday. He brought bags of salt home and set it on the springhouse floor. When the springhouse burned, the salt fell into the spring.'"

With much to tell and the Longs as an audience, the farmers began to vie with one another for the best stories.

"They said how some man came with his spring wagon during the worst of fighting and drove up near the church. There he handed out bread, meat, cakes, and pies that had been sent by some good ladies. Beats me how he ever got out alive!" recounted a red-bearded man.

Another big man laughed and said, "War's not funny, but strange things happen. Women and children were gathered at the Nicodemus farm in the big stone house. Thought they'd be safe there. Then they heard shells screaming overhead and panicked. They were so scared they flew out the front door like a flock of birds, hair streaming in the wind and a line of children of all ages stretched out behind. They stumbled through a plowed field toward the Confederate lines. Every time some-body fell, the others thought it was because of a shot and ran even faster. Rebel Captain Blackford had a good laugh, but being a gentleman, he galloped into the field, swung several small children up on his horse, and led the rest to safety. The Yankees held their fire during the rescue."

The red-bearded farmer, not to be outdone, said, "Oh, did you hear the bee story?" Not waiting for a reply, he continued, "Over on the Roulette farm the Federals drove the Rebels out of the stables and the springhouse at bayonet point. Near the farmhouse was a row of beehives. A Southern shot smashed through the whole beehive. Those bees were in a fury. They at-tacked any and everybody, Blues and Grays. The 132nd Pennsylvania got the worst of it. It looked for a while as if the bees might stop the battle, but the brigade finally got things under control."

Mr. Long, his sons, and his friends had heard enough sto-ries from their neighbors. They were ready to move on and see for themselves the results of the battle.

As they neared the Miller farm, they stopped in horror at the scene before them. A 50-acre cornfield bordered the Hagerstown Pike and extended south. The corn had been tram-pled until only a few stalks remained. No other part of the bat-tlefield had seen such fierce fighting. The dead lay in rows, their bodies so close together that a person could step from man to man without touching the ground. The ground was strewn with muskets, knapsacks, cartridge boxes, clothing, and dead horses.The field was a sea of blood.

As they gazed in disbelief, their hearts seemed to stand still. Finally they bowed their heads in reverence for those who had given their lives when so young for a cause they had been taught to believe in.

Wanting still to see the little Dunkard church they loved, Mr. Long and the other men drove yet farther down the road.

Travel now became difficult. Their horses slowed and picked their way carefully among the prostrate bodies of the Blues and Grays. The scent of human blood terrified the animals. Horses, too, lay dying with their riders. Cries of pain and suffering rose all around them as the Longs moved through the midst of thousands in their final sleep.

Finally they reached the churchyard. They could scarcely recognize the church. A hundred roundshots and thousands of bullets had pierced its white brick walls. A little group of soldiers stood around it. Wounded and dying were laid out on the simple benches, leaving bloodstains that would last forever on pews and floor. Dust and rubble, fallen from shell holes in roof and sides, covered the floor and furnishings. The big leather-bound pulpit Bible was gone, stolen by a Yankee soldier.*

This was the church dedicated to peace and goodwill and that belonged to worshipers committed against slavery and war.

The men fell on their knees and wept.

Shades of pink, of orange, of yellow and robin-egg blue in the setting sun cast a warm glow over the countryside as the men drove home.

While they were gone, some surviving Union soldiers had left the battle scene and headed north on their horses. They had heard of the Long farm and arrived there in midafternoon. One, Frank Holsinger, brought with him a wounded soldier. Immediately he found a friend in Mother Mary.

She invited them into the big kitchen. Accustomed to nursing the sick and injured in her own family, she quickly set about helping the wounded soldier. Her daughters, too, stood ready to assist.

"Ella, we'll need some boiling water, so set the kettle on the hottest part of the stove," she said.

"Susan, we'll need cloths to wash and bandage these wounds, so try to find some soft clean cloths in the mending cupboard.

"Fanny, look on the top shelf of the cupboard for that old

whiskey bottle. It will help to kill any infection that has started."

The soldier was stretched out on the kitchen couch, weak from loss of blood, but able to smile at them. A shot had gone through his upper arm, leaving two ragged wounds that bled freely.

As Mary Long knelt by his side to examine the wound, she turned to Holsinger, saying, "Frank, you've done well in tying your handkerchief tightly above the wound. Without it he would have lost so much blood we couldn't have saved him. It's good that it's bled out. Now I think we can help him."

Together, they removed the blood-encrusted sleeve and set to work. First, she washed the wounds with a cloth dipped in the boiling water and cooled. Then she poured whiskey into the wounds. After that she prepared a poultice of dried herbs to draw out infection and soothe the pain. Around this she wrapped bandages to keep the poultice in place.

The soldier smiled his thanks, closed his eyes, and rested. They covered him with a warm coverlet and withdrew to another part of the kitchen.

Gathering around the table, they listened as Frank told them about the battle. He spared them most of the horrifying details, knowing that the women could not endure it. Listening with their hearts as well as their ears, they were still grieved. To break the mood of sadness, he began to tell them about himself and his experiences.

"I'm from Pennsylvania," he said. "I grew up near Woodberry and decided to seek my fortune in the West. In Kansas I became a sheepherder. It was a great life—lots of wide open space and only hard work during the lambing season. The trouble was the farmers didn't like us. Our flocks were 'free range.' That means we didn't have fences because pasture was poor and the sheep had to find grazing where they could. When we needed them, we'd round them up with horses and dogs and bring them into the corral. The farmers had fences, but didn't keep them repaired. Sometimes our sheep would get in their fields. They started lawsuits against us and ended up wiping me out. I didn't know what to do next, so I came back East and joined the Union army."

Fanny's eyes were bright as she listened to his story. She had never met anyone who had lived as far away as Kansas. *My, how brave he was to venture so far away,* she thought. *And then to join the army, when he could have stayed away.* Feelings welled up within her—unfamiliar ones, but nice ones! She noted how handsome he was, the curve of his smile, his tousled hair, and his firm step.

"Oh, do tell us more," she begged him eagerly.

Frank gave her a long look before he answered. He hadn't missed her rapt attention and beautiful features.

"Well, that's about it as far as my past is concerned, but I didn't tell you everything about the last few days. My friend and I took cover in the Piper barn. Our ammunition was gone, and we had no way to defend ourselves. We were hungry and didn't know where to find any food.

"My friend looked around and said, 'There's a chicken.' I said, 'Where?'

"He said, 'Over there.'

"I caught the chicken, killed it, and hid it under my uniform jacket. That night I roasted it in the campfire. It was the best chicken I ever ate!"

They all laughed, but none as heartily as Fanny.

As their eyes met, Frank knew he had another story yet to tell.

"Just before we left the field, a sentry tried to stop us. I ignored him. He yelled 'Halt' a second time. I still didn't pay any attention. Finally, he called 'Halt!' a third time, 'or I will shoot!' Then I looked at him and said, 'If you want to shoot so bad, just go over the hill, and there you will find plenty of shooting.'"

"Oh, dear," Mary Long interrupted, "we've been so busy listening to your stories we forgot how hungry you must be."

Quickly the women laid out food and drink for the soldiers. It was a pleasant and happy occasion on a day filled with tragedy.

Cassie and Mandy huddled in a corner of the big kitchen, eager to share their discoveries.

"Did you see the way he looked at her?" Cassie questioned in a whisper.

"I sho nuf did," Mandy replied. "I think they be really sweet on each other."

"I thought it was just sickening," Cassie said with a look of disgust. "Fannie was acting ridiculous, staring and laughing so loud at his story. I'd never act like that!"

"He's awful old. I don't know why she'd want him," Mandy said thoughtfully.

"Oh, she just thinks he's a big hero or something. Why, I wouldn't marry a soldier, somebody who killed people."

"I don't think your father would like that much either. 'Course, maybe they'll never see each other again."

"I hope they don't!" Cassie answered with a toss of her head.

Frank and the other soldiers retired to the barn and the hay-mow for the night. The wounded man slept peacefully all night on the kitchen couch.

After breakfast the soldiers prepared to leave. The wounded man would stay until he was strong enough to travel.

Quietly Frank drew Fanny aside and invited her out on the porch. Blushing but willingly she followed him.

As he reached for her hand, he looked her in the eyes, gazing up at his.

"Fanny, you're the prettiest girl I've ever seen. I know you're young and your parents may have other ideas. I hope I can win them over to my thinking if they do. But after this terrible war is over, I mean to come back. I won't forget you. I'll be back to marry you."

Fanny knew she had never been so happy.

Cassie and Mandy had not missed their disappearance, but

Cassie

had sneaked upstairs to watch from a half-open window.

"Wait till Mother hears this!" Cassie exclaimed as they bounded downstairs.

---

*It was not returned until December 1903.

CHAPTER 8

Mr. Long and Melvin had arrived home just at sunset the evening before. They thought they had never been so tired. The fatigue of plowing the field was nothing compared to the melancholy exhaustion they felt after seeing the remains of the bloodiest battle in American history. Father's face was ashen. He had nothing to say and could scarcely place one foot in front of the other.

A worried frown creased his wife's brow. She knew better than to question him at all. Instead, she simply set food and drink before them, in hopes it would lift their depression. They barely touched their food.

As Melvin noted the wounded soldier, he turned his face away. To him, the soldier's presence was yet another painful reminder. He had to have air, get away. Maybe the animals would be some comfort, so he headed for the kitchen door.

Ella broke the silence as she stated matter-of-factly, "Some soldiers are staying in the barn tonight. They're Union men, and they're going north."

Melvin paused, but made no response. He'd go to the stables, mingle with the animals. Maybe he could avoid the soldiers.

Father rose from the table wearily. Facing his wife for the first time, unsmiling and eyes glazed from the memories, he said, "I need to rest. I've seen too much."

His footsteps were slow and labored as he trudged up the stairway to his bedroom.

Mother Mary looked from one person to another. "No family altar! That has never happened. I've never seen your father looking so bad. A long night's rest will do him good. Sleep will soothe his spirit."

The next morning the family arose early. Mother Mary was right. Rest and the forgetfulness of sleep had brought healing to both father and son. Further healing would come with action. They were ready for the day and what needed to be done.

At the breakfast table Father told something of what they had seen. "The loss of life is too great to imagine. The suffering and pain are heartbreaking. We can only go and do our small part to relieve suffering and comfort the dying. First, we'll take all the food you can gather. It's in short supply. Melvin, you and Joseph fill some milk cans with springwater. We can carry those out on the battlefield. Girls, cloths for bandages will be useful. I'm sure there will be some hospital service today, but not nearly enough. As soon as all the supplies are on the wagon, we'll be off."

Cassie had been listening intently. She could only imagine the scenes her father described. Her short life had seen little of pain and death. Conflicting thoughts raced through her head. Could she endure the sight of blood, the stench of the dying, and the cries of pain? Part of her said, *No, I can't stand it.* Another voice inside of her said, *But you must. You want to grow up, be a help during this dreadful suffering. If you don't go, you'll still be a child, thinking first of yourself. But if you do, you'll know you gave all you could.*

Looking directly at her father, she said in a quiet, firm voice, "Father, I want to go too and help wherever I can."

An expression of loving concern on his face, he studied her. "My daughter, do you know what you're saying? It's no place for a young girl. The sights will sicken you."

"Yes, Father, I know it will be very hard for me, but not as hard as the pain of those who are hurting and dying with no one to comfort them. I will learn to be strong. I must go," she said in a final, determined voice.

Remembering her request to attend the slave auction, Father was thoughtful. He knew Cassie's strength of will. How could he deny her the experience of mercy?

"Then find out if Mandy will go with you," he said. "You can help each other."

Quickly Cassie hurried off to find Mandy. She was sober and subdued as she discussed the trip with her friend.

"Father said I should ask you to go along. You don't need to if you don't want to. I don't expect you to feel the way I do. But Father thinks we could help each other."

"Well, I jus' soon go along as stay here all day without you," Mandy answered. "I don't know how I feel. Maybe they don't like a colored girl helpin' them."

"If I were really thirsty, I don't think I'd care who brought me water. I think I'd just be grateful," Cassie replied.

With the wagon loaded with supplies, the four found seats and set off down the road toward the battlefield once again.

As they neared the Miller cornfield, Father urged the horses faster, not wanting the girls to see too much. Today, men were digging huge trenches. Neighbors and soldiers worked together with shovels to bury the dead. Union soldiers were not only burying their comrades but Rebels as well. There were not enough Confederate soldiers left to bury their own.

When they arrived at the church they found a medical staff already there, organizing for surgery.

The little black stove in the church had been fired up for heating water. Steam escaped from large kettles of boiling water. It would be used to cleanse the men's wounds and wash off the makeshift tables after operating. Window shutters had been removed and doors ripped from their hinges to serve as makeshift examining tables. By laying them across pews the physicians could care for many soldiers at one time.

Mr. Long looked at the scene, no longer disturbed by the damage to the church, but seeing it now as a place to relieve misery and give comfort to the dying.

Turning to Melvin and the girls, he said, "They are taking care of the men here. We must go out and minister to those in the fields and woods who have no help. But we'll leave most of the cloth here for bandages. They'll be needing it here after they clean their wounds and operate."

They drove out toward the West Woods just behind the church, offering bread to the hungry as they moved slowly along. Hearing cries for water, they brought the horses to a standstill. Using tin cups or the soldiers' canteens, they answered the pleas for water. Many of the men were sick and feverish. The water relieved their parched throats.

The insistent cries kept the four going. They could not deny a simple call of thirst.

At one point they saw a small group of soldiers around a campfire. The men were making coffee and preparing food to eat, seemingly unconcerned about the suffering around them.

"How can they do that?" Cassie asked. "Why aren't they giving aid to others?"

"It is the way of war," her father said. "Tomorrow may be their last day. They need to gain strength for battle."

At another place two Mississippi brothers were locked in a last embrace, one propped against a tree with a mortal wound, the other by his side, already gone.

A Massachusetts man propped the head of a wounded South Carolina soldier, then drained his own canteen of water by pouring it into the canteen of the injured man.

As the morning wore on, Cassie and Mandy became more and more exhausted. Many times each girl had to stop, hold a hand over her mouth, and choke back the sickness that wanted to engulf her. Other times they went to the wagon, covered their faces, and cried for the sadness they saw all around them.

One extremely young soldier looked at Cassie with such pain-filled eyes that she stopped for a moment. His eyes seemed to beg her to stay. She felt herself torn. Should she stay by his side, or continue to carry water to the many other dying soldiers? Father urged her on to take care of the thirsty men.

By noon wagons and carriages started arriving from Hagerstown. Many people had traveled far to look for sons and brothers. Some realized when they came that their loved one was no longer alive. One man knew his brother had been killed, then buried by his comrades near Lower Bridge with his sword by his side. The brother offered $10.00 to anyone who would find the body. Mr. Fry, a longtime resident, had seen the burial. He led the brother to the spot. The man was able to return home with his brother's body.

Many of the relatives wanted to move an injured man to a house against the doctor's orders. At times the physical effort proved too much for the stricken soldier and he died.

Mr. Davis of Gardner, Massachusetts, received a message that his brother was wounded. Coming right away to look for him, he found him sitting up against a big oak tree. When he spoke to him, he received no answer. The brother was already gone.

While some were arriving from the North and the South to look for their sons, fathers, or husbands, at the same time whole families were leaving the area. They had been robbed of all their food. The Confederates desperately needed horses. A Mr. Neikirk had 11 horses that he had hidden along Antietam Creek behind some rocky cliffs. The Rebels first tried to burn his barn to make him tell where the horses were. When he wouldn't disclose where he had hidden them, they demanded money. His daughter had hidden their money, so he gave them only a little silver. Angry at their failure to get anything from him, they hung him up by a leather halter to force him to tell where the horses were. His son, George, cut him down just in time to save his life.

Cassie

Finally, on the evening of September 18, the Confederates raised a flag of truce at the Dunkard church, only asking for time to tend to their dead and wounded. Since the Rebels were already moving across the Potomac, the Union soldiers had to take care of them.

In the words of a Dunkard poet, James A. Sell:

> "In primal days this house was built
>   Wherein to worship God.
> Within this refuge young and old
>   In solemn silence trod.
>
> "The weary souls on Sabbath days
>   Came here for peace and rest.
> They sang their songs in solemn strains
>   And found their souls were blessed.
>
> The clouds of war o'ercast the land
>   And armies marshaled here,
> And 'midst the din and clash of arms
>   They faced the battle drear
> When cannon belched their redhot breath
>   And poured their shells and balls,
> The sentries found a hiding place
>   Behind its sheltering walls.
>
> "The warhorse left his cruel scars
>   Upon this shrine of peace,
> That mutely pleads in plaintive tones
>   For strife and war to cease.
> The ones who stand for peace on earth
>   And freedom for the slave,
> Will, in better days to come,
>   Be called the true and brave.

"This temple now in ruin lies
    Upon a lonely hill.
The influence of its day and time
    The world can never kill.
Its storm-tossed roof and shattered walls—
    Memorial of the past—
Are pointing to a better day,
    When peace shall reign at last."

Cassie had worked tirelessly all day. When the milk cans of water were empty, the men refilled them at the church well. Many of the wounded soldiers had had no water since before the battle. All day the Long family and others carried water. At first they counted how many men they served, then they were too weary to keep track. It had to be in the hundreds.

By late afternoon Mr. Long decided it was enough. They could do no more. Instead they would come again tomorrow. The girls, too tired to hold up their heads, stretched out on the floor of the wagon, letting their exhaustion overwhelm them at last.

Would life ever be the same again?

CHAPTER 9

Cassie awoke with a heavy heart, the sun already up and shining brightly. Slowly she climbed out of bed. Preoccupied with her thoughts as she pulled on her clothes, she decided she would follow her heart and her duty. She could not forget the pain-filled eyes of the young soldier she had seen the day before. Neither could she shake off his pleading look. Now she knew what she must do.

The family was already seated around the long breakfast table. Only Cassie's chair was empty. Quickly she splashed cold water on her drawn face and slipped silently into her seat. She sought some comfort in the morning prayers.

Each person at the table had heard reports of what they had found on the battlefield. But in the midst of all the suffering, there was some good news to share. Mother Mary could restrain herself no longer. With a quiet smile, she said, "I've heard there's a wonderful woman named Clara Barton who came with medical supplies from Washington. She left on Sunday, driving a covered wagon pulled by eight long-eared mules. Then she set up tables behind the lines so that she could help the wounded as soon as the battle was over. That takes a very brave woman."

"Yes, I've heard about her, too," Melvin said. "She had medical supplies ready before the battle even started. Someone said she was nearly killed. There were more than 300 wounded men lying on the ground outside the Poffenberger barn. She and a Dr. Dunn were trying to get provisions unloaded. One of the wounded men asked for water. While she was holding a cup to his lips, she felt a twitch of her dress sleeve. A bullet went through her sleeve and through the soldier's chest. He died in seconds. But she didn't even stop. Instead, she ordered as many wounded men as possible to be carried into the barn to protect them from stray shots."

"And that wasn't all," Fanny added. "They tell me right after that, a soldier pointed to a bullet in his cheek. He said it was terribly painful and would she take it out. Not being a nurse, she said she'd call a surgeon. But he said, 'No, no, I'll have to wait my turn. You can do it. There's a knife in my pocket.'

"Then another wounded man said he'd help, so he held the soldier's head while she cut out the bullet and bandaged the wound. I shiver at the very thought."

"It seems every barn around here is being used as a hospital," Mr. Long commented. "They're saying fresh air helps the boys recover—that they do best in open air and better in barns than houses because of the air flow. Of course, barns are bigger, too, and doctors can get around better. I've heard that they put the wounded in both the house and the barn at Sam Poffenberger's. They cut up all the bed clothes to make bedding for the soldiers. Then they opened up all the straw and feather ticks and spread the straw and feathers over the floor and over the ground to take care of more patients."

"It seems there's not enough of anything," Ella said. "I heard they used up all the sheets in the houses near the battlefield for bandages. That still wasn't enough. A lot of men are bleeding to death. Now they're using green corn leaves to dress wounds."

"Girls, we can certainly help there," Mother Mary suggested. "We have lots of extra sheets. Let's rip them into strips and send them along with the wagon."

"That's good, Mother Mary," her husband said, "and if you have more bread baked, we'll take that, too. There's just not enough food to keep them alive."

"Oh, how dreadful!" she exclaimed. "Let's think what more we can do. We have lots of cornmeal. We could use cornmeal to make some hot gruel. It will be cold when you get there, but you could heat it in a pot on the church stove. Why not take a bag of dried beans? We don't have time to cook them before you go, but you could divide them up to cook over some of the campfires."

"Mother, I believe we could get a batch of pies finished before they leave," Ella said thoughtfully. "Susan and I can make them in a hurry. I'll fire up the stove right away. It must be just terrible to be in pain and hungry at the same time."

"And another thing," Mr. Long said as he rose from the table. "When we come home tired after a long day, other people, especially doctors and hospital stewards, keep on working, some of them all night. They need light to work. We'd better take as many lanterns as we can round up. Candles are getting scarce, and they aren't safe anyhow. Lanterns give a steady light. In one barn the hay caught fire from candles, though I think they stomped it before it got a good start. With all those men in a barn, I hate to think of the horror if one caught fire."

Sensing the urgency, each one bent to his or her appointed task. Even little Julia ripped sheets into bandages.

Cassie had listened quietly as everyone talked. *Oh, to be as brave and kind and good as Clara Barton,* she thought. *She sounds like an angel. How can she be so strong? I could never cut out a bullet. I would probably faint away, but I'd love to meet her! Of course, she'd be too busy to notice me. Anyway, I will find Mandy and see if she wants to go along today. Probably not. I think she had enough yesterday. I won't mind if she doesn't. She might not like it if I spend all day with one person.*

Tossing back her braids, Cassie hurried off to her barn chore. Being in a serious mood, she gave the lambs but passing notice, eager to finish her chores and get back to the battlefield.

As she and Mandy walked slowly back to the house,

Cassie turned to Mandy, asking, "Will you be going to the battlefield today?"

"I don't think so. It was real bad yesterday. I felt sick most of the time. And I was so tired I could barely sleep. Some of them soldier boys called me names! I'm not used to that now. I didn't like it at all. I thought it was mean."

"I'm sorry, Mandy. I know that must have hurt you a lot. It's just what they're used to. I didn't hear them or I would have told them that you're my friend and not to talk that way to you. They would probably have laughed at me, but I wouldn't care. I wonder if they will ever learn?"

"It is gonna be a long time. That's what they always hear, and they think they are better than us. They won't change soon," Mandy said.

The two friends entered the kitchen arm in arm.

"Come join us; we can use more help," Mother Mary said to them. "We'll soon use up all the sheets, but then all these strips need to be rolled into bandages."

"Sure, we'll be glad to," Cassie said. "It looks like fun."

They were soon busy. Sometimes a bandage would slip from too-swift fingers and unroll itself across the wood floor. The cat, snoozing complacently by the fire, would perk up its ears, eye the moving object, and pounce on the roll in ecstasy. The children laughed at it.

The bandage rolls were soon packed to go. Cassie had chosen some extra-soft cloths for her own use. Bathing a feverish brow would require the softest of cloth as well as a gentle hand.

Together with Father and Melvin and a wagonload of supplies, Cassie set off once again for the battlefield.

When they arrived at the little bullet-scarred Dunkard church, Cassie gathered her supplies together. Warm water, a basin, soft cloths, bandages, drinking water, and a bag of food. She was prepared for her day.

Mr. Long looked at Cassie with questioning eyes.

"Father, I won't be following you on the wagon today," she said in a firm voice. "There is a special person who needs me. He's so young and so lonely. I will stay with him as long as he needs me." In a quivering voice, she continued, "He may not make it another day. He needs somebody by his side."

As he looked at his daughter with gentle eyes, Mr. Long said, "Cassie, you're growing up. You're not a child anymore. I'm glad you've made your choice. You are beginning to have the feelings of a woman. It won't be easy for you, but it is good that you follow your heart."

As she picked her way carefully across the field, Cassie studied the faces of the men who lay all around her. Not heeding their pleas and closing her mind to their suffering, she stared ahead, her brown eyes darting from face-to-face, searching for the one she could not forget.

Already hardened to the grim sights of a battlefield, she plodded on, until—*Yes, there he is,* she said to herself. Smaller than most, with light-brown curly hair, a ragged ill-fitting gray uniform and eyes closed, he lay motionless.

With a sudden little cry, she rushed forward, quickly kneeling beside him. In fevered haste she undid his jacket. Reaching inside his shirt, she laid a hand on his chest. *Thank God, his heart is still beating. Oh, what shall I do first? Water, that's it! Every soldier needs water.* She filled a cup. Lifting his head with one hand, she held it to his parched lips with the other. A few drops at first, and soon slow swallows. Then she paused. Maybe she had given him enough for now.

Slowly, his eyelids fluttered open. He looked at her, not quite able to focus. She smiled as she gently held him.

"Who are you?" he asked slowly.

"I'm Cassie, your friend. I live on a farm near here. I came today to help you and stay with you."

"You are kind," he answered, trying to rise. "My name is

James. I'm from South Carolina. I've been hurt bad. I don't think I'll make it home again."

Exhausted, he sank back. Cassie found a soft cloth and bathed his feverish face. Pushing back his tousled hair, she stroked his brow with the soft cloth.

As he rested, Cassie's eyes observed each detail of his young face. He was too young to shave. Only a few stray bristles showed on his chin. His still-baby-soft skin was smudged with blood and dirt. Carefully, Cassie washed away the grime. Then lifting his hand, she washed and stroked it.

Opening his eyes again, James spoke in a slow, barely audible voice.

"I need you to write a letter. My mother will want to know. She didn't want me to leave. She said, 'You're too young.' I'm only 14, you know. You'll find what you need in my knapsack."

Cassie unbuckled his knapsack. There she found a few sheets of paper and a stubby penknife-sharpened pencil.

"I have some warm soup, James. Would you like some before we begin the letter? Maybe it would make you stronger."

"I'm not hungry, but it might help. You're so kind."

Quickly Cassie found the still-warm soup. Carefully she pressed spoonfuls of soup to his lips while holding him in a raised position. Swallowing was difficult at first, but became easier as Cassie waited patiently. She knew he had been without food for several days. Some strength began to return to his pain-racked body.

"That's enough," he said finally. "Perhaps later I will be ready for more. I feel stronger. We can start the letter."

Pausing frequently for breath and strength, for most of the morning hours he struggled to tell her what to write.

Cassie wrote in painstaking sentences, filling in the missing words to shape a letter for his mother. Between times she ministered to his needs with sips of water or gruel and by bathing his flushed face. Joy filled her heart when he was able once to smile and look into her eyes.

"You are an angel sent from God," he said. "I will die happy because of you."

Cassie squeezed his hand and touched his brow.

When he closed his eyes, she raised his head and slipped her arm under it as a pillow while kneeling close to his side.

"I'm ready," he whispered at last.

Tears streamed down her checks as she said, "Goodbye, and God bless you, James."

A few short breaths, and his head relaxed in her arms. The end had come.

Cassie sat holding him for several moments, tears dripping onto his face. Finally, she laid his head back on the ground and folded his arms across his body.

Now, what shall I do? I can't leave him here. I wonder where Father is. Glancing around the battlefield, she saw the wagon approaching, and hurried to tell her father.

"Please, Father, you must come, and we must leave. James is gone and we can't leave his body here any longer. He must have a proper burial."

"But, my daughter, who is this James?"

"He—he's my friend, a Rebel who was only 14 years old and now he's dead," she said through her tears.

Mr. Long drove the wagon close to where Cassie indicated. Following her lead, Mr. Long and Melvin found the young boy. Together they carried him to the wagon.

"Oh, Father," Cassie asked, "can he be buried in the family plot? I know his uniform is gray, but does it matter?"

"No, Cassie, we are all brothers, and since he meant so much to you, we will bury him with our own."

"Thank you, Father," she replied gratefully. "You see, he asked me to write a letter to his mother, and now I can finish his story. Would you like to hear the letter that I wrote for him?"

"I'd be honored," her father said as he rested quietly.

Hands shaking and voice trembling, Cassie read:

" 'Dearest Mother,

"I am thinking of you now, as I have constantly since I left you. Your tears when I left broke my heart, but I knew I had to join my comrades. If only I could spend one day with you now, I would be so happy. My short life is almost over. I have been mortally wounded. My leg has darkened and the poison is creeping through my body. So much pain has left me weak. There are doctors and nurses here now, but they are too late for me. So many men have died already. Many more, like myself, were wounded. Cassie, a friend who is with me now, has promised to mail this letter to you after I'm gone. She is very kind. She will stay with me until I breathe my last. She will send you my knapsack with my few personal effects. You will be comforted knowing I did not die alone. I'm so sorry to bring you more grief. You were always a wonderful mother. I'll love you through eternity. We will meet again in heaven.

Your loving son,
James' "

"Isn't that beautiful, Father?" Cassie said softly as her eyes met her father's steady gaze.

"Yes, Cassie, it is a beautiful letter from one so young. You loved him very much, daughter, didn't you?"

"Oh yes, very much!" she said in a half whisper.

On the way home each was absorbed in private thoughts. Cassie was sad, yet strangely joyful in the assurance of having given herself fully. *Will life ever be the same again? No, I'm sure it won't. I am no longer a child. James died for a cause he believed in. I will live to bring comfort to others.*

CHAPTER 10

When Cassie awoke late the next morning the sun was again high in the sky. Her head ached, and she didn't want to move. Anguished thoughts began racing through her mind, though she was barely awake.

Why, oh why must there be this terrible war? James was too young to die. How did he feel, knowing he'd never grow up, never have a wife or a child of his own? Oh, what pain he must have suffered! Still, he didn't complain. He said it was hard for him to shoot but he was willing to die because he had snuffed out the lives of others. James felt it wouldn't be right for him to live. Adding to his torture were the cries and groans of those all around him that he was unable to help.

I wouldn't have left him. I would have stayed the night on the battlefield by his side. He had no meanness in him. I'm glad I could give him a little comfort in his last hours. I will always remember him.

Pushing back the covers, Cassie pulled on her long stockings. Then she slowly slid her blue homespun dress over her head. Her long brown braids were wet with her tears. Bits of dried blood and dirt from the battlefield clung to the ends. Cassie undid the braids mechanically, then grasping her wire hairbrush, she vigorously brushed through her long thick hair.

I'll leave it loose today, she thought. *Clean air blowing through it will freshen it and take away the battle smell.*

After pulling up her bed covers, she trudged down the back

stairway and unlatched the door to the kitchen. There gentle smiles and a circle of warm understanding eyes greeted her. No words were necessary. It was wonderful to have a caring family.

After finishing a bowl of oatmeal that had been kept warm for her, Cassie headed out the door. Mandy came tripping up the path.

"Oh, Cassie, can you believe it? We have a new lamb. The mother seemed so restless last evening that I thought her time was near. I ran out to see early this morning, and he was already trying to stand up. My, but he was wobbly! He seemed like all legs."

Together they hurried off to the barn. Cassie rushed into the sheep pen. When she saw the new black lamb, she fell on her knees close enough to cuddle him. Stroking his rough, springy new wool coat, she looked into his liquid eyes. As he let out a lusty little bleat, she smiled happily and studied his small black face.

"Oh, he's so adorable," she exclaimed. "I wish he'd never grow up."

The mother sheep crowded close, baaing protectively.

"It's all right, Susie," Cassie said to her. "I love him almost as much as you do. I'd never hurt him."

The mother sheep nudged the baby lamb, but seemed to sense that Cassie would not hurt him.

Mandy stood by, smiling broadly, proud of her discovery.

"What shall we name him?" Cassie asked.

"Oh, it's easy," Mandy replied. "He's black and the others are white. His name just has to be Blackie."

The friends nodded to each other in agreement. Releasing the lamb and helping him to his feet, Cassie and Mandy watched as he searched for his mother's milk. Soon he was suckling noisily.

"I think babies are sent from God," Cassie said. "It doesn't matter if they're human babies or animal babies. They're so innocent and helpless and pure. And they remind us of God's love."

"I think you are right," Mandy agreed, nodding.

The girls left the lamb pen and walked hand in hand toward the house. Mandy broke the silence with a ripple of laughter.

"Oh, I did hear the funniest story, Cassie. A soldier stopped at the house yesterday while you were gone. He was hot and asked for a drink of cold water. Mama Sally sent me to the spring for a bucket of water. I brought it to the front porch where he was sittin' and waitin'. I gave him a dipperful, and then he said, 'Let me have that dipper. I bet I could down that whole bucketful. Seems to me I've been thirsty for days.'

"After he had enough, Ella brought him some bread and meat. I guess that made him feel like talkin'. Anyways, he started telling stories.

"He said, 'Ya' know Squire Miller's place.' We all nodded our heads that we did.

" 'Well,' he said, 'he had a parrot in a cage that hung on the back porch. On the battle day a shell burst in the air nearby. One of the pieces cut the strap that held the cage. As the cage dropped to the porch floor, the parrot said, "Oh, poor Polly!" ' "

The girls had a good laugh.

"Mandy, you always make me feel good. I don't know what I'd do without you," Cassie said. "You know, I really wish I could see Clara Barton. Do you think Father might take us over to her hospital today?"

"I sure don't know. But you won't find me going with you. Too much blood! I'd sooner take care of little Orville."

"It's all right. I don't blame you. It's just that I've heard so much about her. I think she must be the greatest woman there is. I'd do 'most anything to see and meet her. I can't bear to go back to the Dunkard church today."

The door banged behind them as the girls entered the kitchen. Father still sat at the breakfast table.

"You must be very tired," Mary Long said as she looked lovingly at her husband.

"Yes, it wears both body and spirit. It's the tiredness that saps all the get-up-and-go in a man. Still, there is so much to do," he answered in a strained voice.

Cassie walked to the table and, looking her father in the eyes, said evenly, "Father, I can't go back to the church today. Would you—could you take me to Clara Barton's hospital instead? I'd so much like to see her. You could help there, too."

His eyes brightening, Father said, "Why, that sounds like a good idea. I've heard that she and her workers set up a hospital at the Poffenberger farm. It won't be far to drive. Maybe we can learn more about caring for the wounded. Is Mandy coming with you?"

"No, she'd rather stay here. I don't mind. I will just be so happy to see Clara Barton. Maybe she'll even let me help her."

An hour later the wagon with Mr. Long, Melvin, and Cassie arrived at the Poffenberger farm. They drove up the lane amidst the devastation of battle. Heading for the barn first, they halted the wagon just outside it. Inside the barn, lying on beds of hay and arranged in rows side by side, were several hundred soldiers. A woman moved quickly from one to another, carrying a pail of hot soup and a dipper. To each one she offered a dipper of gruel. Many times she knelt by the soldier's side, lifted his head with one hand, and patiently tipped the ladle to his lips with the other. A smile and kind words accompanied each serving of gruel.

Cassie watched, entranced. The woman seemed so beautiful and efficient. She moved so quickly, but gave each man both food and attention. It had to be Clara Barton.

Without hesitation Cassie stepped quickly between the men until she reached her. Pulling at her sleeve, she managed to get the woman's attention.

"You must be Miss Barton. I want to help you. I've heard

how much you've done and how hard you worked. Will you let me take your place for a while?" Cassie asked eagerly.

Obviously surprised at seeing a young girl, Clara Barton smiled as she looked into Cassie's excited brown eyes. "But of course you can help, dear. Some of these boys aren't much older than you are. There are so many needs to be met."

The men had gone to the house where doctors were amputating and treating many wounds. There they assisted in this most painful of tasks.

Women helpers in the basement of the house stirred large iron kettles of gruel over an open fire. Taking turns in transporting full buckets of hot soup, they made sure that Clara had food for her soldiers.

People were still coming and going, looking for sons, brothers, and husbands. Cassie became a message bearer as she sought information from the officers to relay to the soldiers' relatives.

Later she heard that one woman, a Mrs. Fields, had come from Ohio, having been notified that her husband was ill with typhoid fever. Arriving at midnight with food for her husband, she learned that he had died two days before and was buried. She wept bitterly over his grave. The next day she returned home with his cap and a few of his small keepsakes, including a photo of her and their two children.

Cassie heard equally sad stories from the different helpers. Two grandsons of Paul Revere from Massachusetts had lost their lives at Antietam. One, a doctor, was treating wounded soldiers in the West Woods and died in action.

Cassie noticed that Clara Barton never paused to rest. She worked until she was totally exhausted or until she had run out of supplies. In spite of her weariness, she always had a smile and a kind word. *No wonder they call her an angel,* Cassie thought. *She never thinks of herself.*

As they journeyed home in the near darkness, the girl felt tired but contented. She had met a great woman and had worked beside her. It had been a memorable day.

Rising early the next morning, Cassie enjoyed a warm breakfast of cornmeal mush with honey and sweet cream. She did not mind that meals were simpler than in the past. She appreciated each mouthful as she realized how many hungry soldiers there were.

Today she would spend at home with Mandy. Many of the wounded were being moved to the Smoketown Hospital. The men would go and assist with this difficult task.

It was a beautiful late summer day and nothing would suit her better than a carefree romp in the woods.

As she headed for the door, her mother called, "Cassie, I'd like you and Mandy to watch Orville today. Some fresh air will do him good. He's been inside so much and under our feet constantly. We'll get more done in the house if you take him for a walk."

A small frown creased Cassie's brow. That wasn't a part of her plan. Orville was always wandering off, trying to chase a squirrel or discover a rabbit in hiding. Today, all she wanted was a secluded grassy spot where she could talk with Mandy for hours. They had so much to discuss.

I guess they do need a break, she thought. *I don't know why Fanny can't take him. She's not that much older than I am.* Mandy came bounding up on the porch and saw Cassie's frown. "What's wrong?"

"Oh, we have to watch Orville today, and you know how he is. He'll never let us talk two minutes," Cassie said glumly.

"Yeah, I know. He doesn't stay still even a minute. 'Course, if we have to, then we have to."

Reluctantly, they invited Orville to go for a walk with them. He trotted cheerily toward them. Together they headed for the woods.

Orville raced ahead as the girls picked their way through the cutoff cornstalks. Sharp on the tops, the stiff stalks could cut or injure. Several times Orville stumbled and fell forward in his eagerness to reach the woods, but he picked himself up without help. Engrossed in their talk, the two did not notice how far Orville had gone until a cry caught their attention. They hurried to Orville's side. He had not been so lucky this time. Pointing to blood flowing from a cut, he wailed loudly.

"Why, Orville, you cut your leg on that ole cornstalk," Cassie said. "No wonder you're crying. It must really hurt. We must do something to stop that blood."

Mandy pulled a clean cloth out of her deep dress pocket. "Here's my handkerchief. Let's try wrapping it around his leg."

Orville watched wide-eyed as the girls carefully wound the cloth above and around the cut.

"It has to be tight to stop the blood," Cassie explained, "but not tight enough to hurt. Does it feel all right, Orville?"

The child nodded soberly.

Satisfied with their bandaging, the girls resumed their conversation.

"I think boys must be terribly brave," Cassie said. "I've seen lots of them who never cry or make a sound when you know they're hurting bad."

"Yeah, I don't think I could stand what they do. I'd just faint away," Mandy replied.

"And they're strong, too. Melvin lifts these big bags of feed by himself. I can't even lift half a bag."

"I'm glad I'm a girl," Mandy continued. "I'd much rather cook and work in the garden than do men's work. I like being 'round the house. Horses are smelly, and men walk behind a plow all day. What a bore!"

Idling along dreamily, the girls barely noticed that they had left the fields and entered the woods. Crunching through fallen leaves, they began looking for a resting place. The woodsy coolness was pleasant and a welcome change. Birdcalls and skittering wildlife only enhanced the stillness. Cassie stopped abruptly.

"Oh, my goodness, Mandy, we've forgotten Orville. I don't see him. Where might he be? Which way did he go? He could have gone toward the creek. What shall we do?"

"We got to find him!" Mandy said with determination. "We was just enjoying ourselves too much. It looks like a path here to the left. I'll follow that while you go lookin' toward the creek. He can't be too far."

Off they went in separate directions.

Terrified, Cassie ran toward the creek. *I'll never forgive myself if anything has happened to him,* she thought. *How could we forget!* She ran wildly. Reaching the stream, she surveyed it upstream and down, taking in the middle and each side in one quick glance. No signs of a little body. Thank God! He didn't seem to be around the creek. Now where?

Cassie dashed back to the spot where she had left Mandy. "Mandy, do you see him?"

"Not at all, Cassie," came the other girl's voice, "and I've looked and looked."

The girls met again, not knowing what to do next. They looked at each other with a mix of guilt and fear. No sign or sound of the boy. Where could he be? They tried to think. The woods gave no answer. Wait! What was that sound?

They listened, hope and uncertainty vying with each other. Was it really—? It was! That was a child's cry. They tore through the underbrush heedless of scratches and torn clothing. Now the cry was louder and more desperate. Was Orville hurt? What had happened? Soon they were kneeling by the trembling little boy.

Exhausted from crying, the child had stretched out on the warm leaf bed. His foot had caught under a thick root, and he had not been able to get free. Frustration had mingled with the terror of being alone.

Gathering him in their arms, the chastened girls retraced their steps toward home. Thankful for his safety, they showered him with attention.

Maybe I'm not so grown up after all, Cassie thought. *I can't even take care of my 2-year-old brother.*

Later, when Orville proudly showed his mother his cut leg, she frowned and raised questioning eyes to the girls.

"Just an ole cornstalk," Mandy said, looking away.

CHAPTER 11

Five days after the battle of Antietam the Longs heard that more than 23,000 young men had been killed, wounded, or missing in one day.

Chores followed the usual ritual, for less of everything merely meant a return to frugality, something not unfamiliar to the pious Dunkard family.

Sitting around the breakfast table, they discussed plans for the day.

"I still have some grain to take to the mill," Mr. Long said, "and I'll pick up some supplies at the store. I know you womenfolk have been running out of things when you send food to the soldiers. It's been good of you, taking on this extra work. Let me know what you'll need, and I'll try to get it. We still have some meat and garden vegetables to barter."

"The flour and cornmeal are low, and we'll need woolen cloth and sewing thread for fall sewing," his wife answered. "The girls and Mama Sally have made provisions go a long way. I'm beginning to understand how Jesus fed the 5,000 with a few loaves and fishes."

A chorus of laughter followed her comparison.

"I'll be leaving shortly so that I can spend the afternoon in the fields," Father said. "Let me know if there's anything more you need."

Still feeling bad about losing her brother Orville, Cassie

said, "A piece of licorice would be nice for the little children. It costs only a penny."

"I think I can manage that," Father answered, his eyes twinkling.

Soon after noon Cassie heard a clatter of horses' hooves. As she stood on the front porch, she saw the horses pulling the wagon at a fast trot. Why? Usually they plodded slowly home after a long drive to the mill. As they came closer, Cassie saw a broad smile on her father's face.

Mr. Long brought the horses to a sudden stop, made a quick leap from the wagon, and as quickly tied the reins to the hitching post.

"Wonderful news," he called. "Ring the dinner bell. Everyone must hear it at once!"

Cassie hastened to give the bell rope three strong tugs. Farm and house workers alike dropped their chores to heed this emergency call. Anxious looks first and then smiles enveloped their faces as they saw Mr. Long's joyful look. They quickly assembled on the front lawn and waited in respectful expectation.

"Today will long be remembered in history," Mr. Long began. "It is the beginning of a new era in our country. It has just been announced that President Lincoln issued the Emancipation Proclamation. That is, he declares free as of January 1, 1863, all slaves in the states that are in rebellion against the federal government."

Shock and disbelief appeared on the faces of each grown-up. In a short time excited chatter replaced it. Cassie and Mandy, though wordless, grabbed each other's arms and danced about with joy. Pausing briefly, Cassie said, "Now there won't need to be any more fighting. The war will be over."

Mandy, excitement mounting, shouted, "Praises be! There ain't gonna be war no more!"

Only the grown-ups understood the great differences in the North and the South and how difficult it would be to resolve them. To them, it was a great step forward, but with many events to follow.

Almost two weeks later, on the afternoon of September 30, two wounded Union soldiers rode onto the Long farm on equally battle-worn horses. One horse was limping badly and the other had been partially blinded by gunpowder. The first soldier, Mel, wore a tattered blue uniform with one sleeve flapping free where the now amputated arm had been before the battle. Robert, the other soldier, now walked with difficulty, having been shot in the thigh. He was one of the fortunate ones. A surgeon had removed the bullet, and the wound was healing nicely. The Long farm seemed a likely place to find shelter for the night.

Encountering Mr. Long as they rode down the lane, they stopped.

"Good day, sir," Mel said. "We're headed north to Chambersburg. It's rough going, and we're worn out already. We're looking for a place to spend the night."

"Stay and welcome," Mr. Long answered as he eyed their injuries. "Better to take it slow than to aggravate those wounds. Go on up to the house and tell the women that I sent you. They'll know what to do."

That evening after supper the Long family and the two visitors sat around the fire in the living room. The men discussed the week's events as the women listened while doing their needlework. Cassie strained to catch every word.

"There was some excitement in the air today as we traveled up the pike," Robert announced. "Rumor has it that President Lincoln will be arriving tomorrow. Some say he's unhappy with General McClellan. Too many men killed and too slow to move."

"I've heard that, too," Melvin added. "The men seem to like 'Little Mac' and his little horse, Dan, well enough. Trouble is, he's afraid to give orders. I hear the battle was fought by divisions, no united effort."

"If President Lincoln does come, he'll see the waste of life," Mr. Long commented. "It wouldn't surprise me if he found a replacement for McClellan. He wants this war over as much as any of us."

"Most of the Confederates really hate Lincoln," Mel said. "They call him an ignorant backwoodsman. People on both sides talk about how homely he is. They blame him for starting the war."

"It's a man's job, being president," Mr. Long replied. "When a man takes a stand on anything, people take sides. He's only doing what he has to do to save the Union. I think he's shown great courage."

Cassie's eyes opened wide. *President Lincoln coming here? We may even have a chance to see him. He can't be as ugly as some people say. The man is too kind and good.* A daring thought entered her mind. "Oh, Father," she interrupted, "do you think we might go to see him tomorrow? We may never have another chance."

"It would be a high honor to be in the presence of a great man like Mr. Lincoln," he answered. "We can try, but not knowing how and when he's traveling, we may easily miss seeing him. Those that want to go will need to be ready to leave by 8:00 in the morning."

Cassie was jubilant. She couldn't wait to tell Mandy. Even though it was late and already dark, she dashed out of the house and raced to Mandy's cabin.

"Oh, Mandy," she said as she burst through the door. "You'll never guess. We can go to see President Lincoln tomorrow! We must be ready early in the morning."

"Whoa, Cassie," the other girl interrupted. "What you sayin'? How we see Mr. Lincoln? He live in Washington, D.C."

"But he's coming here—to Sharpsburg—tomorrow, and Father said we can go."

"Ya mean it? It's for real?"

"Of course! Why else do you think I ran all the way here to tell you?"

Mama Sally, suddenly alert, asked, "Do you mean all of us can go?"

"Sure, everyone that wants to. That's what Father said."

Realizing the lateness and that she'd soon be missed, Cassie hurried back to her house.

She could scarcely contain herself as she sat through their regular family worship. The songs, Scripture, and prayers seemed to be hopelessly dull this evening and endless as well. Later, it took quite a bit of time for her to fall asleep.

Rising early, the women were more quickfooted than usual. A sense of urgency filled the kitchen. Eyes were bright as they anticipated this out-of-the-ordinary event.

Breakfast over and cleared away, the family started out the door to take their place on the spring wagon waiting by the gate. To their surprise, all the Black help had assembled on the front lawn, ready to join them.

With some pushing and squeezing, they were soon all in two wagons and off for a gala holiday.

Crimson and gold-leaved trees, floating clouds in an azure sky, and a soft breeze added to their delight on this first day of October. The horses trotted willingly along the Hagerstown Pike, now badly damaged by the battle.

As they drew closer to the scene of battle, they found people on horseback and on foot, all hoping for a glimpse of the president. Soon a crowd was milling about in the churchyard and along the road. The news had spread like a grass fire, so that people left home before dawn to see their gangly president. Some had brought food and drink, prepared for a long wait.

Shortly before 11:00 someone saw dust on the road to the east. Voices became louder. Eyes strained to see. Was it really Mr. Lincoln or just a country wagon?

At last they saw coming toward them a barouche, a four-wheeled carriage, drawn by six white horses wearing red, white, and blue plumes on their heads. A uniformed soldier rode each horse.

The carriage with a folding top had a driver's seat in the front and two double seats inside and facing each other. Mr. Lincoln sat facing the front. Five invited guests accompanied him. Easily recognizable in his tall beaver hat, the president held up his hand. Eyes about closed, he faced the crowd with his slow, sad smile. The carriage halted near the little bullet-ridden church and the great man rose and stepped from his carriage.

Cassie, close by, noticed the dusty carriage and remembered his long ride. Rushing over to the church well, she pumped water into a large dipper. Carefully, she carried it to the spot where Mr. Lincoln stood talking to several bystanders.

"Would you like a cold drink of water, Mr. President?" she asked politely.

"How thoughtful you are, little miss," he replied. "I'm exceedingly thirsty and would love a cool drink."

With that, he reached for the dipper and emptied it in seconds.

As he returned the dipper to her, he placed his large hand on her head and smiling, said, "God bless you, my child." Holding it there, he expressed to the hushed crowd his regret for the damage done to the property of "you good people."

Cassie felt she might die of happiness. It was truly the greatest day of her life. As she looked at him, she saw a beautiful man, not ugly at all. True, his beard was scruffy, he had bushy eyebrows, thick lips, and deep lines in his face, but those deep-set eyes showed kindness greater than she had ever known.

After inquiring the whereabouts of the nearest hospital, someone directed Mr. Lincoln to the little church.

Taking long strides, his thigh-length black coat flapping behind him, Mr Lincoln soon entered the shell-torn, blood-stained church. The old-fashioned pulpit, the unpainted pine benches, and the rough plaster walls were stained with dried blood. Before him on a number of pews were lying wounded young men in tattered gray uniforms, Confederate soldiers left behind as their comrades retreated south.

Mr Lincoln greeted them and said that if they didn't mind, he would be pleased to take their hand. Addressing them further, he said, "We owe solemn obligations to our country. Our children's future requires the prosecution of war. Many of us are enemies by circumstances. I bear you no malice."

After several quiet moments, those who were able to move about came forward and shook hands with their president. He urged the wounded to be of good cheer and assured them they would receive the best possible care.

From there the barouche and six horses headed for General McClellan's headquarters.

The Long family was subdued on the return to home and work. It had been a great day. Now they must move forward with the spirit of Mr. Lincoln.

CHAPTER 12

The air was brisk, but just enough to be invigorating on a sun-drenched October day. Some leaves had fallen, but the woods and orchard were ablaze with autumn colors.

"What a perfect day to be outside! I love this kind of weather," Cassie said as she and Mandy headed toward the orchard.

"It really be a nice day," Mandy replied. "Twon't be long until the leaves go and the cold comes."

"Yes, and then we're stuck inside most of the time. That's the worst! Winter seems to go on forever."

"This one will be 'specially long with food so scarce," Mandy added sadly.

Not wanting to talk about that, Cassie changed the subject. "Mother said she needed apples picked, so let's."

"I'll get the basket by the springhouse," Mandy offered. "We can fill it, and that should be enough for pies and some to eat."

Soon the girls had settled themselves in the grass munching apples and talking before tackling the apple picking.

"If the army camped on your farm and took most everything, which would you rather they leave, a horse or a cow?" Mandy asked.

"That's a tough one," Cassie said thoughtfully. "I guess a cow, because we'd have milk to use and she'd have plenty of grass to eat. Then if a neighbor had a bull, we could probably have a calf in nine months, and in another two years we'd have another calf and more milk."

"You really look ahead." Mandy laughed. "Sounds all right, but what about plowing? How are you gonna have any crops? You need a horse for plowing."

"In olden times I believe they used cows to pull plows. Maybe it was a special kind. I don't know. They were called oxen. At least, we could try hitching a cow to a plow."

"You really be funny," Mandy said. "'Magine Old Bessie pulling a plow! She'd roll her eyes and get right contrary."

The girls mused about this possibility. Unaware that 7-year-old Julia had followed them, they were shocked when a sudden yell broke the silence.

"Help me! I'm falling!" came a desperate cry from the direction of the apple tree.

Then they saw that Julia, ever the venturesome tree climber, was high up in the tree. Holding on with one hand, her one foot on a thin, bending branch, Julia was groping for another handhold or a sturdier branch to stand on. Neither seemed to be within reach. She had climbed too high and now had panicked as the slight limb began to shake.

"Cassie, Mandy, help me!"

The girls dashed to the foot of the tree. Looking up, they saw a terror-stricken little girl appearing to dangle from the treetop. Her dress had caught on one limb, one foot hung loose, and another rested on a small quivering limb.

Mandy's eyes widened. Soberly, in a half whisper, she said, "She gonna fall!"

Grabbing hold of some low branches, Cassie pulled herself up into the tree. "Hang on, Julia. Hang on tight. I'm coming!"

Cassie continued her climb, choosing sturdy limbs for footholds. It was slow progress with her long dress catching on each small branch.

"Hurry, please hurry!" Julia begged. "The branch—it's breaking!"

Sure enough, Cassie heard a menacing cracking sound.

She climbed faster until she was almost in reach of the girl. *If I can just grab her hand,* she thought, *I'll pull her toward me.* It was a risk, she knew. They could both fall.

A step higher. She tried to reach the girl. Not close enough yet. Julia's hand was still six inches away. A huge step, and Cassie made one frantic pull upward. Steadying herself, she groped for her sister's hand. With a loud cracking, the little branch supporting Julia's foot snapped from the tree. In the same split second their hands met. Clinging frantically, Julia fell against her big sister, who had braced herself against a strong limb.

Julia's small body shook as she broke into tears. Cassie reassured her with gentle pats. As Julia's fright gradually ebbed, Cassie began the slow descent. Holding her sister's hand and grasping safe branches with the other, she carefully guided the child downward.

When they reached the ground safely, Cassie's tension eased, but other feelings burst to the surface. "Don't ever do that again, Julia!" she scolded. "You could have been killed. We didn't even know you were here. Why did you climb so high?"

"I don't know. I just like to climb. But not anymore, I don't. It was too scary!"

"Well, I won't tell if you promise not to try a stunt like that again."

"I promise," Julia answered meekly.

Two weeks had passed since the last service in the little Dunkard church before the great battle. It would be months before they could meet in the battle-scarred building again.

The Long family rose at dawn on Sunday, eager to finish their chores quickly. By 8:30 Cassie and Mandy were seated on the front porch steps in their go-to-meeting clothes, scarcely able to repress their excitement.

"It will be so great to see everyone in meeting again today," Cassie said. "It wasn't easy to call everyone together, but Father thought it was time we do. I guess we'll need to meet here for Sunday worship for a long time."

"I glad it's a pretty day like yesterday," Mandy said. "Everyone likes eating outside. It would be real crowded inside."

"There'll be a lot less food than the last time," Cassie said seriously. "Some people hardly have any left. I know they'll bring what they can."

"We be real lucky. The meat that Ella and Susan hid away will help a lot. And they made lots of applesauce yesterday."

"It will be nice to be together. Our farm looks better than most. The menfolk have been working hard to get things repaired and crops taken care of. I can hardly wait!" Cassie said, hugging herself.

"They're coming! I hear them. Let's go meet the first wagon," Mandy exclaimed.

Off the two girls ran. Soon they returned, out of breath but smiling as wagons rolled one by one toward the house.

Mother Mary, Ella, Susan, Fanny, Lizzie, and the little ones crowded onto the front porch, eager to meet their friends. The men were soon milling about in the front yard. There was much hand-shaking and warm greetings. Gradually they made their way in through the open door.

Rooms had been cleared, chairs arranged, and benches supplied so that they could hold an orderly church service. Soon everyone had gathered in the spacious house, seated themselves, and waited quietly for it to begin.

Church service began with a period of hymn singing. An elder announced the hymn, lined it, and the congregation sang. Joy rose in everyone's heart from this shared experience. Reading of Scripture, comments, and a lengthy prayer followed as the people knelt.

Elder Long stood and paused until everyone had again

seated themselves quietly. Looking into the faces of each one present, he began:

"Brothers, sisters, boys, and girls, we are here together after two weeks that we will long remember. We have survived. All have suffered loss, some more than others. I don't know if anybody ever wins a war. I think the beginning of this war has been fanned by hate until it's a blaze now, and a blaze can destroy the one who starts it as well as the one the fire was set to hurt. There ought not to be a war. This war ought never to have been. We are a union. Separate, we're just weak, puny pieces, each needing the other.

"Now we will need to pick up the pieces of our lives. We will not forget the horrors of the battlefield, the blood, the pain, the lost sons, and the grieving families. These scenes are imprinted on our minds forever. Let that pain drive us forward. We will rebuild our homes, our barns, and our land. We will reach out in helping each other. And we will share our horses and wagons, our grain and foodstuffs, so that nobody need starve. In this, God will bless us and we will reclaim that which is rightfully ours."

Elder Long continued at some length, adding appropriate scriptures to strengthen faith and give hope to all those assembled. At the end he called for prayer. Fervently he prayed, first giving thanks for their lives, their unity, and then he sought answers for their needs. Many eyes were tearful, but a gentle peace settled on the group.

After dismissal, the women quickly headed for the kitchen. The men went outside, where they discussed their losses and how they could help one another.

"Brother Sam, we all know you've lost everything. How can we be of the most help?" one of the men questioned.

"I want to rebuild as soon as possible," Sam Mumma replied. "The Sherricks have been good to us, inviting us to share their home and their food. But it is an imposition to stay longer than we have to. I'll go to the bank tomorrow and try to arrange for a loan. There are trees in our backwoods for lumber. I'll plan to start cutting on Tuesday. Extra hands will be of great help."

A chorus of "I'll be there's" followed his announcement. The discussion continued as the farmers assessed their needs and organized for work.

Joyfully, the women carried food from the kitchen to the improvised tables outside. The people sat down and someone asked a blessing. The food was not bountiful, but well prepared.

After the meal, the men continued their discussions, presenting their needs and seeking answers to problems.

Cassie and Mandy helped in clearing the tables and putting away the dishes. Little food remained.

"I guess they don't need us here anymore," Cassie said. "I saw the older girls walking out toward the ball field. Shall we go, too?"

"Sure, I'd like that," Mandy replied.

Hand in hand, they strolled toward the ball field. Chatting and laughing together, they seemed not to notice anything else. Fanny and Lizzie along with several other older girls had already arranged themselves demurely on the grass under the big hickory tree. In half whispers they shared secrets with frequent furtive looks toward the ballplayers on the field. Occasional soft laughter rippled among them. Cassie and Mandy held their heads high disdainfully and looked elsewhere as they passed by the little group.

"I do think they act so silly," Mandy commented. "They don't fool me. I know what they're talking about. Boys! Boys! Boys! That's all they ever think about."

"I'm never going to act dumb like they do," Cassie answered. "Did you see Fanny's face? The redness started on her neck and just moved right up her face when she was talking to her friend, Cora. I bet it was about that soldier, Frank. She'll be mighty disappointed if he doesn't show up again."

"She certainly will. She's countin' big on him. 'Course, I guess we can't blame her. She'll be old enough to marry by the time he gets back. Let's sit here under the maple tree."

The girls plopped down on the grass with a clear view of the playing field.

The game had not yet begun. The boys were still determining sides. Finally, concluding they had too few players for a game, they glanced toward the older girls.

"Anyone over there want to play?" Mahlon, the tallest boy and obvious leader, called.

A tittering of laughter flowed through the group, followed by vigorous headshakes.

Mahlon looked uncertain, then gave a half-glance toward Cassie and Mandy. That's all they needed. "We'll play," Cassie declared.

"Oh, all right, if you're not afraid of getting smashed," he answered.

The girls dashed onto the field, very aware of their long skirts. They wound up on opposing teams. The game began.

Soon Mandy came to bat. Steeling herself, her eyes focused on the ball, she waited. One ball, two balls, three balls. None of them seemed right to her. On the fourth her eyes gleamed as she gave a hard swing and connected. The ball hurtled out between second and third base.

Cassie, being closest, ran to catch it. For a split second it was in her hands. Then, to her dismay, it as quickly dropped to the ground. A chorus of jeers around her nearly brought tears. *I've got to try harder,* she thought. *I can't let them do this to me.*

Mandy was a fast runner and made it to first. A fourth player was up to bat. On the second throw he swung. Again the ball hurtled Cassie's way. Determined, she stood her ground, cupped her hands, and closed in on the ball. Mandy was running fast toward second base. Cassie threw the ball to second, putting Mandy out and retiring the side.

"Yeah, Cassie!" sounded over the field, and Cassie suddenly felt inches taller. *I did it,* she thought. *Now they won't trample me.*

The game continued, the girls holding their own and exulting inside as they sensed acceptance from the boys.

As the game ended in a tie, Cassie and Mandy ran toward each other, hugged, and dashed off the field. "Let's see what the grown-ups are up to," Cassie said. "It looks like they're gathering for a meeting before people go home. Let's find out what they plan to do."

The girls hastened toward the adults assembled in the yard, finding a spot on the grass at the back of the group. People continued to roam about and talk in an animated manner. At the same time a feeling of closeness and unity was evident as they discussed the future. Finally, voices subdued, the women found seats on benches or chairs and the men settled themselves on the grass.

Elder Long stood before them. "Brothers and sisters, our hearts are warmed because of our fellowship together today. We have suffered together, and now we have drawn strength from each other. And we will move forward together. What's done is done. There are many broken families in our midst, so much suffering. We cannot undo what man has done. It is a tragedy that must never happen again. Tomorrow is a new day. We will put our hands to the plow and bind up the wounds of body and soul. Our God will show us the way."

He raised his hand and uttered a brief prayer of thanks and blessing on each one present, then finished with an echoing "amen."

Reluctantly and quietly, these devout German Baptists walked toward their wagons, homeward bound. A clatter of hooves and a rumbling of wagon wheels signaled the end of despair and a new beginning.